COFOUNDER OF BEAD

SIMPLY
STUNNING
JEWELRY

A TREASURY OF PROJECTS,
TECHNIQUES, AND INSPIRATION

POTTER
CRAFT

NEW YORK

Published in the United States by Potter Craft,
an imprint of the Crown Publishing Group,
a division of Random House, Inc., New York.
www.crownpublishing.com
www.pottercraft.com

POTTER CRAFT and colophon is a registered trademark of Random House, Inc.

Portions of this work were originally published in the following:
Simply Pearls by Nancy Alden, copyright © 2006 by Nancy Alden, photographs by Joseph
De Leo, photographs copyright © 2006 by Potter Craft, a division of Random House, Inc.
Simply Silver, Simply Gold by Nancy Alden, copyright © 2007 by Nancy Alden, photographs by
William Brinson, photographs copyright © 2007 by William Brinson
A Touch of Glass by Nancy Alden, copyright © 2008 by Nancy Alden, photographs by Jennifer Lévy,
photographs copyright © 2008 by Potter Craft, a division of Random House, Inc.
Simply Gemstones by Nancy Alden, copyright © 2009 by Nancy Alden, photographs by Jennifer Lévy,
photographs copyright © 2009 by Potter Craft, a division of Random House, Inc.

Library of Congress Cataloging-in-Publication Data is available upon request.

ISBN: 978-0-307-46459-0

Printed in China

Series Design by Lauren Monchik
Design by La Tricia Watford

10 9 8 7 6 5 4 3 2 1

First Edition

CONTENTS

SUPPLIES & FINDINGS

JEWELRY MAKING SUPPLIES

Before you rush out to buy any of the items listed below, carefully read the list of necessary ingredients and tools for the project you have in mind. Some require few tools or materials. In recent years, the proliferation of bead stores around the world has made it easy to acquire jewelry making supplies. If you do not have a local bead store, there are numerous mail-order suppliers, most of which offer online shopping.

TOOLS

It's surprising how few tools you need to make jewelry. For many necklaces and earrings, you can get away with just two: a pair of flat-nosed pliers and wire cutters. The other tools you need to make the designs in this book are detailed in "Toolbox Essentials" on the following page.

Some of these items you can find around the house, but you'll want to make a modest investment in tools specifically designed for jewelry makers because they will make your life easier and your finished jewelry better.

There are other specialty items you can add as you go along, but the items in "Toolbox Essentials" are all you really need. Some people like to lay out their necklaces on a bead design board that has specially designed curved channels for holding beads. If you don't want to purchase one, you'll need to work with a bead mat or some other thick, soft material to keep your beads from rolling all over the place.

Like everything in life, beading tools come in levels of quality. Their cost depends on precision, sturdiness, and durability. If you are on a budget or think that your enthusiasm for making jewelry might be short-lived, you can buy cheap pliers to get yourself started. When you are hooked by the satisfaction and pleasure of creating your own jewelry, it will be time to upgrade—look for tools made in

Germany. Once a passion for the craft sets in, you might want to splurge on a really superb set of Swedish cutters and pliers. But the important thing is just to get started.

SPACERS

Spacers are just beads that create spaces between other larger or more important beads. Theoretically, all beads can act as spacers. In practice, however, spacers tend to be fairly simple silver and gold beads, although they are sometimes more elaborate. Their most important characteristic is that they should emphasize, rather than overwhelm, the main beads. Spacers do not always do this by being restricted in number: sometimes they are used sparsely, and sometimes they comprise the majority of the design. Nor are they necessarily restricted in beauty. A whole strand of gold daisy spacers, for instance, can be a thing of pleasure. The spacers' position in the design determines their character. Spacers are beads that know when to hold back and let others take the central role.

STRINGING MATERIAL

The main structure of a neck "lace" is, by definition, a piece of thin material that can be wrapped like a lace around the neck. This material can be silk thread, leather thong, wire, chain, or one of the modern bead-stringing wires. Whatever the material, it must combine both strength and flexibility. Here are the stringing materials we recommend.

SILK

This traditional material is still preferred for threading beads and designs where the thread is to be knotted between the beads. It is reasonably strong, easy to work with, and very, very supple. While modern beading wire is stronger and easier to use, no other material allows a strand of beads to embrace the neck in quite the same way as silk. But silk has some distinct disadvantages: it will break when roughly handled, it will stretch over time, and it gets dirty. Because of this, any beads strung on silk will have to be restrung periodically. How frequently depends on how much you are wearing them. But a good rule of thumb is that necklaces that are worn regularly should be restrung every one or two years.

Silk comes in several thicknesses, which are expressed by an arcane alphabetical code. The thickest silk thread is FFF, while the thinnest is size 00. For our projects that require silk thread, we are going to use size F and keep things simple.

BEADING WIRE

Modern technology has tried to overcome the disadvantages of silk, while retaining its qualities of flexibility and ease of use. This was a surprisingly difficult task and the only material to come close is a relatively new and sophisticated product. Beading wire seems simple: it's just a few twisted strands of wire coated in plastic. But early attempts were frustratingly inadequate. The wire was too stiff to lie around the neck gracefully; it would kink if bent sharply and it would break if mishandled. The problems were solved by twisting more and more strands of thinner wire to add both flexibility and strength. Today's 19- and 49-strand beading wires are increasingly kink-resistant; they don't break under normal use and, although still not quite as supple as silk, they are very flexible. With the logic of an industry more used to hardware than jewelry, the manufacturers of beading wire have decided to measure its thickness in inches. This completely ignores the fact that the holes in beads are measured in millimeters. Wherever "beading wire" is called for in the materials list we recommend using the best quality 49-strand size .015. If a thinner or thicker wire is called for, it is specified in the materials list.

CHAIN

Whatever style of chain you prefer, I recommend that you use only sterling silver and gold-filled. Plated chain is cheaper, but deteriorates quickly and is not an appropriate material to use with gemstones. Solid gold chain is, of course, nice to have, but very expensive. In appearance and durability, gold-filled chain is the next best thing.

WIRE

Stringing beads together with wire is easier than it first appears. In these designs we use just two types: sterling silver and gold-filled, both in a "half-hard" density. Wire is sold in another traditional measurement, "gauge." The wires used in these designs are either 20 or 22 gauge, corresponding to .032 and .025 of an inch.

TOOLBOX ESSENTIALS

- Wire cutters
- Narrow flat-nosed pliers (also known as chain-nosed pliers)
- Round-nosed pliers
- Awl (for designs on silk thread)
- Crimping pliers (can be used instead of flat-nosed pliers to close crimps on beading wire)
- Scissors
- Beading needle (twisted wire)
- Hypo-cement glue (or clear nail polish)

FINDINGS

These linking pieces are the jewelry maker's essential hardware. Just as the carpenter fills his toolbox with the nails, screws, and bolts needed to construct his works, so the jeweler has her stock of clasps, wires, and links. There are hundreds of different findings, but you need know only a few to make the jewelry in *Simply Stunning Jewelry*. Most findings come in different metals, and you should always use the one that is appropriate to the design. The basic materials are listed below.

FINDINGS FOR NECKLACES

BEAD TIPS

Bead tips attach the end of a necklace thread to the clasp. The tip is designed to grip onto the knot you make after stringing the last bead, and it comes in two varieties, the basket bead tip and the clamshell. The former works by trapping the knot in a little basket, while the latter sandwiches the knot between two concave wings that look like clamshells.

CLASPS

Clasps for necklaces and bracelets come in a staggering variety. Several different methods are used to attach the two halves of a clasp, but all the styles are attached to the necklace pretty much the same way.

CRIMPS

Crimps are tiny metal beads that can be crushed flat with pliers. Beading wire is first threaded through the bead crimp, then through the loop of a clasp, and then back through the crimp. Finally, the little crimp is firmly but carefully squashed to attach the wire to the clasp. There is even a specialty tool, crimping pliers, that helps exert the right amount of pressure to make a perfect seal. You can also close crimps with simple flat-nosed pliers.

CRIMP COVERS

These provide an easy way of disguising the messy part of the necklace between the clasp and the first and last beads. They are hollow spheres that open up like clamshells. You simply fit them over the flattened crimp and squeeze them gently shut. Once in place, they look just like a smooth round silver or gold bead. Although these findings are not necessary for the construction of a necklace, they can add an extra touch of sophistication to your designs.

FINDINGS MATERIALS

GOLD use only with gems, pearls, or beads of high value.

GOLD-FILLED use with any good gems, pearls or beads.

VERMEIL (STERLING SILVER PLATED WITH GOLD) use with modest-value gems, pearls or beads.

NIOBIUM (HYPO-ALLERGENIC METAL) use if you have an allergic reaction to silver.

SILVER (STERLING OR BETTER) use with real pearls and beads or gems of good quality.

PLATED BASE METAL use only with the very cheapest materials.

STYLES OF CLASPS

- Hook-and-eye
- Fishhook
- Box
- Toggle
- Lobster claw
- Spring ring
- Sliding

FINDINGS FOR EARRINGS
EARWIRES

Earrings for pierced ears use earwires designed to fit through the pierced hole. Other earrings use earwires that clamp on to the earlobe with a clip or a screw. Earwires for pierced ears should always be of good quality and made from material that does not cause an allergic reaction.

FINDINGS COMMON TO BOTH EARRINGS AND NECKLACES
HEADPINS AND EYEPINS

These are simple pieces of straight wire on which you thread your beads. The "head" or "eye" at one end keeps the beads from falling off, and the other end is attached to the beading wire, chain, or earwire.

JUMP RINGS, SPLIT RINGS, AND PLAIN RINGS

These findings are often used for linking parts of necklaces and earrings. A jump ring is a simple metal loop that can be opened and closed by twisting. A split ring cannot be opened, but the item to be connected can be slipped onto it by feeding the item around the split in the side of the ring. (Split rings are just miniature versions of the metal rings on key chains.) A plain ring is one that cannot be opened because the ends are soldered together.

FINDINGS KEY

Following Pages

1. Gold-Filled Shepherd's Hook Earwire (left) "Add-On" Earwire (right)
2. Silver and Gold-Filled Crimp Beads
3. Silver Bead Caps
4. Silver Leverback Earwire (left) Earwire with Ball (right)
5. Silver Bead Caps
6. Silver and Gold-Filled Crimp Covers
7. Antiqued Silver Bead Caps
8. Silver and Gold-Filled Basket Bead Tips
9. Vermeil Headpins with Ball Tip
10. Gold-Filled Headpins
11. Silver and Gold-Filled Eyepin
12. Silver and Gold-Filled Rings
13. Silver Jump Rings
14. Silver and Vermeil Headpins with Ball Tip
15. Gold-Filled Lobster Clasp
16. Silver and Marcasite Toggle Clasp
17. Vermeil Lobster Clasp
18. Silver Box Clasp
19. Silver and Marcasite Toggle Clasp
20. Gold-Filled Box Clasp
21. Gold-Filled Box Clasp
22. Gold-Filled Lobster Clasp
23. Vermeil Toggle Clasp
24. "Stardust" Silver Toggle Clasp
25. Vermeil Lobster Clasp
26. Silver Hook-and-Eye Clasp
27. Silver Toggle Clasp
28. Vermeil Toggle Clasp
29. Silver Hook-and-Eye Clasp
30. Gold-Filled Three-Strand Sliding Clasp
31. Silver Hook-and-Eye Clasp
32. Gold-Filled Spring Ring Clasp
33. Silver Toggle Clasp

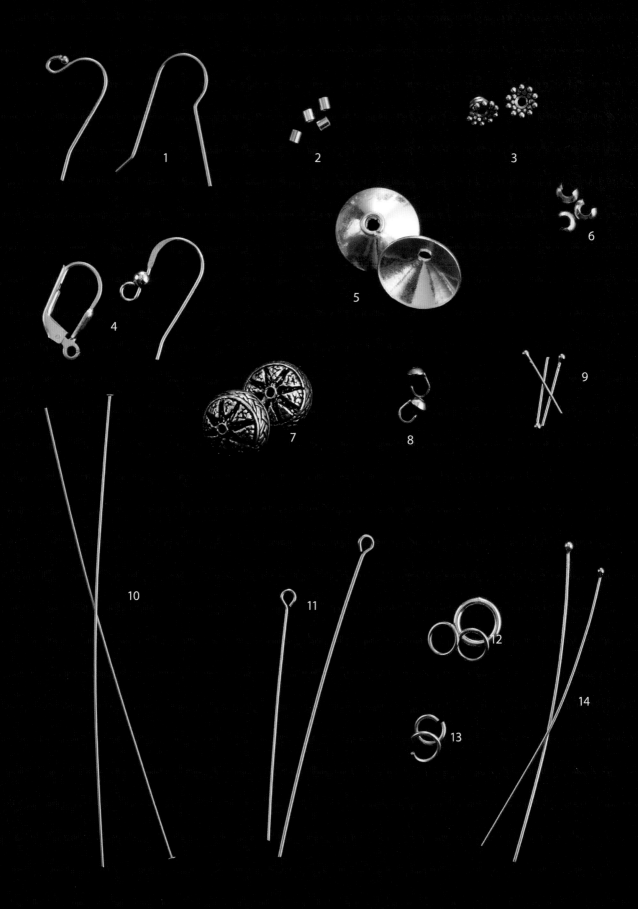

1

2

3

4

5

6

7

8

9

10

11

12

13

14

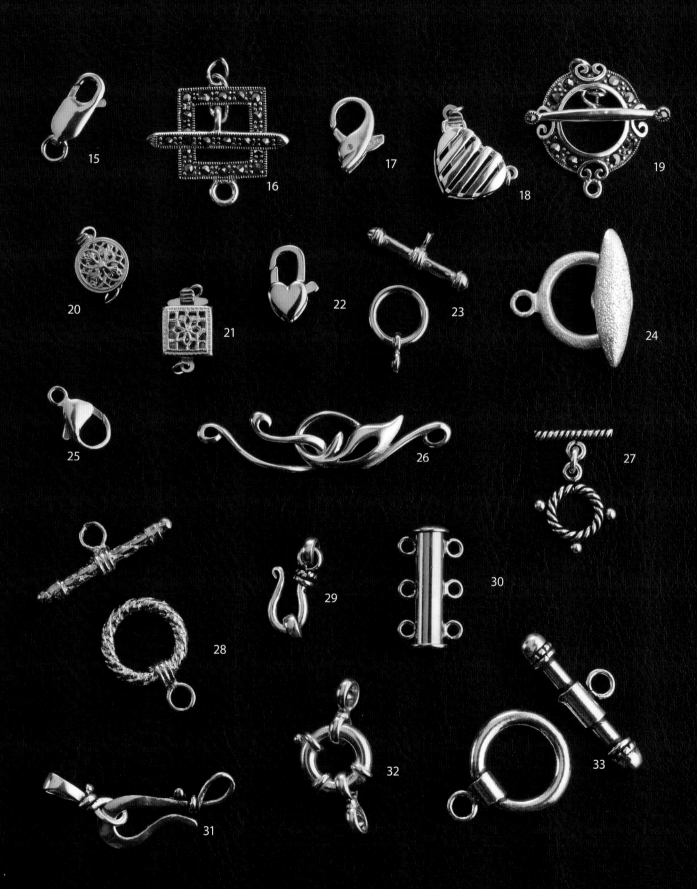

15

16

17

18

19

20

21

22

23

24

25

26

27

28

29

30

31

32

33

TECHNIQUES

BASIC JEWELRY MAKING

During many years as a jewelry maker, I have found that these methods work well for me. More importantly, I have found that they work well for the people I have personally taught and for the thousands of people who have been taught by our knowledgeable Beadworks instructors.

Some of these techniques are simple and require hardly any practice, although dexterity is a big help. Others need patience and several attempts to get right. If you find yourself becoming frustrated, remember that it is mostly a matter of familiarity. If at first you don't succeed, cut the beads off the thread or wire and start all over again!

There are also many bead stores and educational organizations that offer beading classes. If you are the sort of person who learns best through hands-on teaching, they provide a quick way to get started.

To begin working with beads, you need a well-lit, flat, hard surface with some kind of soft covering to stop the beads from rolling around. If you are going to work at a table or desk, you can buy bead mats or bead design boards or simply use a towel. Personally, I prefer to work on my studio floor, which is well carpeted and allows me to surround myself with tools and beads and a cat to keep me company. Have a mirror nearby so that you can check the look and length of your necklaces and earrings.

Good tools make everything a lot easier. I always use two pairs of flat-nosed pliers, one of them with narrow jaws. Your round-nosed pliers should have tips narrow enough to make really small loops. If you discover a love for making jewelry, treat yourself to a really good quality pair of wire cutters.

Once you are seriously into making jewelry, lots of little containers are essential for storing your beads and findings. These can be anything from old jars to specialized bead vials, but it does help if they are transparent and have lids. Multi-compartment plastic boxes are also a great storage method.

THE GOLDEN RULES

The carpenter's maxim is "measure twice, cut once." The wise jewelry maker measures a necklace and bracelet at least twice, and then tries it around the neck or wrist for size. She lays it down and double checks the pattern. Only then does she make the final knot or squeeze the last crimp bead shut. Never finish off your jewelry until you are absolutely sure it is right!

Don't let a little clumsy work spoil the whole piece. If you forgive a bad knot or a missed spacer, you will see the flaw every time you wear the jewelry. Better to start over and get it right.

Don't ruin good ingredients by mixing in poor ones. Even if the material is hidden by the beads or under your hair, use good quality. (Never, ever, string anything on fishing line!)

Assume you are going to make mistakes. I constantly make mistakes even after many, many years of jewelry making! If the pattern calls for two headpins, understand you will need at least two more on standby for when you cut them too short or bend them too badly. If it requires twenty inches of beading wire, make sure you have the rest of the spool nearby for when you need to start all over again.

Don't waste time looking for exactly the bead called for in a recipe. Use a substitute of the same quality with similar design values (color, size, shape, texture). Never pass up a good bead. If you see one you really, really love, buy it, and let it inspire a future design.

USING CRIMP BEADS TO ATTACH CLASPS

Crimps are little hollow tubes that can be crushed together to grip stands of beading wire. You use them like this:

1. Pass the beading wire through the crimp, then through the loop of the clasp and back through the crimp again. With a pair of crimping pliers or flat-nosed pliers, squeeze the crimp until it firmly grips both strands of the wire (Illustrations A, B).

2. Snip off the tail of the wire as close to the crimp as possible (Illustration C).

A slightly more sophisticated finish can be achieved by using crimp covers. These fit over the flattened crimp and are gently squeezed shut to create the look of a normal bead. Note though, that you can only use crimp covers if you have used crimping pliers to flatten the crimp.

Another trick is to hide the tail of the beading wire inside an adjacent bead or beads. I always do this if the hole in those beads is big enough to hold two thicknesses of beading wire, and I often add a spacer bead to the end of my design just to permit this method to be used.

1. Pass the beading wire through one or more beads, then through the crimp and through the loop of the clasp.

2. As you bring the beading wire back through the crimp, push it further back through the bead(s).

3. Squeeze the crimp shut and snip the tail of the wire as close as possible to the last bead it was passed through. In this manner, the tail end of the beading wire will recoil very slightly and be hidden inside the last bead.

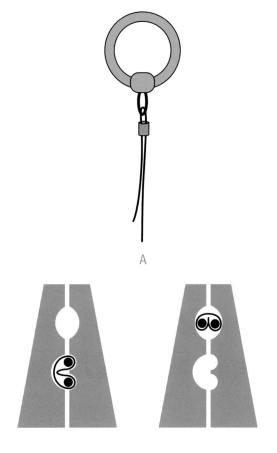

A

B

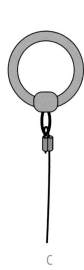

C

USING JUMP RINGS AND SPLIT RINGS

JUMP RINGS

1. With a pair of flat-nosed pliers, grip the jump ring so that it lies flat between the pliers with the join slightly to one side of them.

2. Grip the other side of the join with your fingers and twist the ring sideways so that it opens.

3. After looping the ring through the piece or pieces you are connecting, close it by once again gripping it with the pliers and twisting the wire back until the two ends meet and the join is closed. Make sure that the two ends of the wire are flush with each other.

Never open jump rings by pulling the ends apart as they will be much more difficult to close. Always twist them sideways as described above.

SPLIT RINGS

1. Although there is a specialist tool you can buy to open these, the simplest way is just to slip your fingernail between the split parts of the ring just behind the opening. You should then have created enough of a space to push the piece you wish to connect into the split of the ring.

2. Rotate the ring until the connected item has traveled all the way along the split and out of the opposite side. You may want to use your flat-nosed pliers to help rotate the ring.

GETTING KNOTTED: THE ART OF USING SILK THREAD

Strands of beads are sometimes strung on silk thread, which is thought to offer the best compromise between strength and flexibility. It is best to thread the beads onto a doubled strand of silk, both to add strength and increase the size of the knots. While you can use silk thread without knotting between each bead, it is traditional to knot between them to highlight each bead and to prevent them from chafing against each other.

A

STRINGING ON SILK THREAD

In order to draw the thread through the beads, you need to use a needle. While any thin needle will do, flexible twisted wire needles make the job a lot easier.

1. Thread the silk through the eye of the needle and draw it through until the doubled length is enough for the necklace (Illustration A). If you are knotting between each bead, your doubled strand should be at least twice as long as the finished necklace. For example, an 18" knotted necklace will require two yards or 72" of silk thread [18 x 2 x 2].
    If you are not knotting between each bead, the doubled thread should be about six inches longer than the finished piece. An 18" necklace will therefore require four feet or 48" of thread [(18 + 6) x 2].

B

2. Tie the doubled end of the thread with a simple overhand knot and tighten it by pulling on the tail with your pliers (Illustration B).

3. To tighten the knot even more, separate the two threads and pull apart (Illustration C).

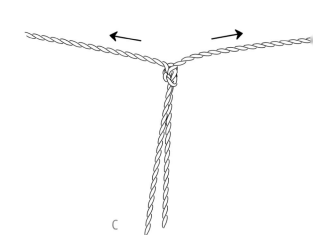

C

USING AN AWL TO MAKE KNOTS:

An awl is a metal needle with a long handle that is used for getting knots to sit up tightly against beads or bead tips. It is very simple to use once you know how. You can use the next step to practice knotting. Once you begin to make a real necklace, you will first have to attach the clasp (see page 18).

1. Add a bead to the thread. Make an overhand knot anywhere along the thread, but do not tighten it. Put the point of the awl through the knot and gently reduce the size of the knot until it fits loosely around the awl (Illustration A). Put your finger on the thread so that the knot lies between your finger and the awl.

2. Now, keeping your finger on the knot, move the awl toward the bead. You should be able to easily move the knot all the way down the thread until it is tight up against the bead.

3. Once you have the knot in position, slowly remove the awl as you pull on the thread to tighten the knot (Illustration B).

4. To tighten the knot even more, you can separate the two threads and pull apart to help force the knot closer to the bead (Illustration C).

5. Add another bead and push it firmly against the knot you have just made, then make another knot as above. Make sure the beads are tightly against one another. Continue practicing with a few beads until you are confident that you have the technique mastered.

TOOLS TIPS

When you need to knot and can't find your awl, fold out a safety pin and use that.

If you've lost your scissors or can't find your cutters, get out your nail clippers. They are usually very sharp and you can get them nice and close to your bead to cut off excess thread or wire.

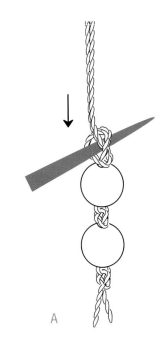

A

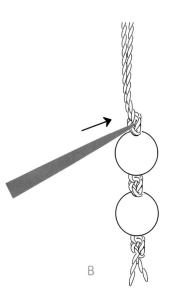

B

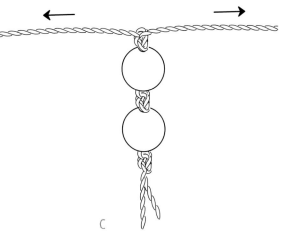

C

USING BEAD TIPS TO ATTACH CLASPS

When you are stringing on silk thread, you need to finish off the ends in a way that will let you attach them to each half of a clasp. The little findings that enable you to do this are called bead tips. One end of a bead tip is a simple loop that will connect to the clasp. The other end grips the knot at the end of your thread.

To use either kind of bead tip, start with your thread doubled and knotted at the end.

STRING-THROUGH "CLAMSHELL" BEAD TIPS

1. Start with your doubled thread knotted at the end. Make another overhand knot on top of the first knot at the end of your thread. This is easier to do if you use your awl to guide the loop of the second knot to a point where it will sit on the first. Tighten that knot as well. Unless you are very sure of your knots, add a dab of hypo-cement or clear nail varnish. Trim off the excess tail of the thread with a pair of sharp scissors (Illustrations A, B, C, D).

2. Pass your needle and thread into the open clamshell of the bead tip and through the hole at the base of the shell. Pull the thread completely through so that the knot sits snugly inside the clamshell. Using flat-nosed pliers, gently squeeze the sides of the shell together so that it closes around the knot and grips it firmly (Illustrations E, F).

3. Make another single knot tightly against the bottom of the bead tip. Now add the beads to the silk thread to create your necklace.

4. Once you have completed stringing all the beads of your necklace, finish it off by passing the needle and thread through the hole on the outside of another bead tip. (Remember to make a knot after the last bead.)

5. Pull the thread so that the last knot of your necklace sits firmly against the outside of the bead tip. Now tie an overhand knot so that it sits inside the clamshell of the bead tip. To position the knot properly, use your awl to move the loop of the knot as close to the inside wall of the bead tip as possible, then tighten the knot, pulling the awl out at the last moment. Make a second overhand knot and tighten it on top of the first. Add a dab of hypo-cement if needed. Using flat-nosed pliers, gently squeeze the sides of the shell together so that it closes around the knot and grips it firmly.

6. Using a sharp pair of scissors, trim off the rest of the thread as close to the outside of the bead tip as possible.

7. You now have a strand with a bead tip at either end. Put the open loop of one bead tip through the ring on one half of the clasp. Use flat-nosed pliers to close the loop so that it is firmly attached to the ring. Attach the other bead tip to the other part of the clasp in the same manner.

TIP

If you add a few smaller beads to the beginning and end of your necklace, it will be easier to undo and close the clasp when you wear it.

QUICK TRICK

If you have an idea for a necklace but don't have the time to make it up, string a few beads defining at least part of the design on a piece of thread or even fishing line and tie off both ends. This way, you will be able to remember what the idea was when you find time to make it.

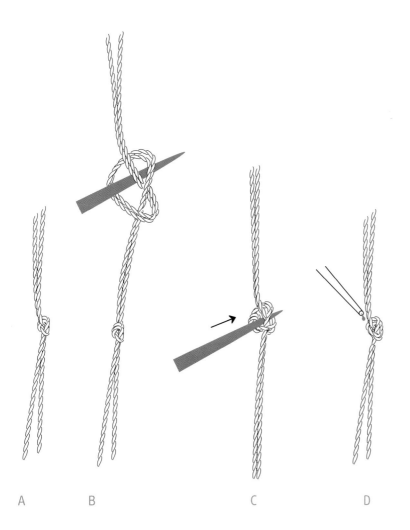

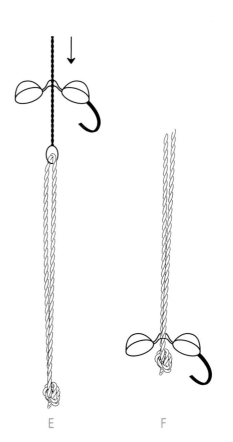

A   B   C   D   E   F

USING "BASKET" BEAD TIPS

While it is a little more difficult to make the final knot in this style of bead tip, they give a more sophisticated look to your jewelry—if you can master the technique.

1. Take the end of the doubled thread and tie a simple overhand knot. Tighten it by gripping the tail with pliers and pulling. Trim off the excess tail of the thread with a pair of sharp scissors (Illustration A).

2. Pass your needle and thread into the inside of the "basket" and through the hole at the bottom. Pull the thread completely through so that the knot sits snugly inside the bottom of the basket. Put a tiny dab of hypo-cement or clear nail polish on the knot (Illustrations B, C, D).

3. Make another overhand knot near the outside of the bead tip and use your awl to move the loop of that knot tight against the bottom of the "basket." This knot will prevent the beads from chafing against the bead tip and improve the overall appearance.

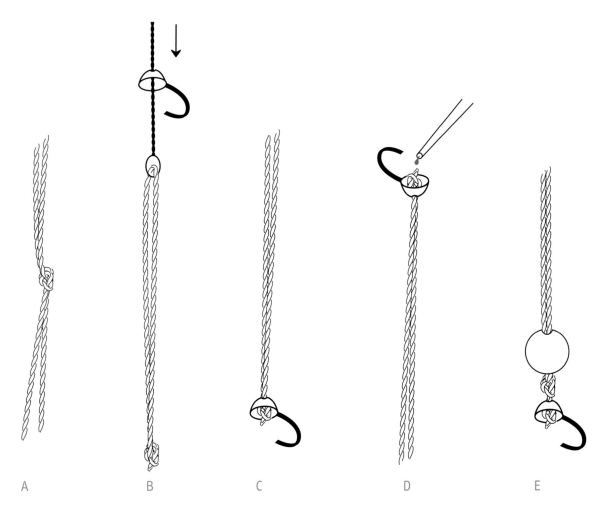

A   B   C   D   E

4. Now add the beads on to the silk thread to create your necklace (Illustration E).

5. Once you have completed stringing all the beads of your necklace, make an overhand knot and use the awl to position it tightly against the last bead. Now pass the needle and thread through the hole on the outside bottom of another basket bead tip. Pull the thread until the bead tip sits firmly against the knot after the last bead (Illustration F).

6. Now tie an overhand knot and use your awl to move the loop of the knot as close as possible to the bottom inside wall of the bead tip (Illustration G), then tighten the knot, pulling the awl out at the last moment. It takes a little practice to get this final knot to slip into the "basket," but it is important to get a good tight fit so that no thread can be seen once the necklace is complete. Add a tiny dab of hypo-cement or clear nail polish to this knot (Illustration H).

7. Finish off by attaching the ends of the bead tips to the clasp as above (Illustrations I, J).

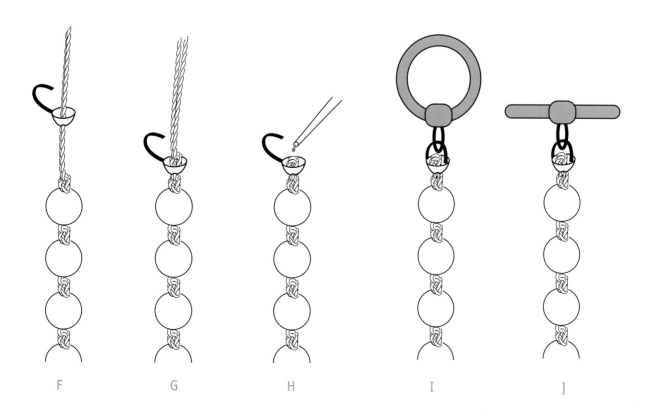

F   G   H   I   J

USING HEADPINS AND EYEPINS

Headpins and eyepins are convenient ways of attaching beads to necklaces, earwires, and other findings. Simply add some beads and make a loop at the top. To make the loop:

1. Hold the bottom of the pin to make sure the beads are sitting tightly against it, and cut the top of the pin to the correct length for the loop. For a 3mm size loop, there should be a quarter of an inch of the pin above the last bead. Small loops are made by gripping the wire towards the tips of the plier's jaws. If you grip the wire further back, the loop will be larger. If the loop is bigger, you must allow more wire between the bead and the end of the pin. When you practice this technique, it is useful to make a mark on the jaws of your round-nosed pliers so that you know where to place the wire between the jaws (Illustration A).

2. Grip the top of the pin between the jaws of round-nosed pliers. Make a "P" shape by rolling the pliers away from you. Move the pliers around if necessary until the tip of the pin meets the wire at the top of the bead (Illustration B).

3. Put your fingernail behind the neck of the "P" where it touches the bead, and bend the loop back until it is centered above the bead. Your finished loop should look like a balloon with the string hanging straight down (Illustration C).

4. To attach the loop to another, open it to the side as with the jump ring below.

NOTE

If you are wire wrapping on a headpin or eyepin, follow the instructions on page 23, substituting the headpin or eyepin for the wire. For larger loops, allow more distance on the wire. Remember the wire's placement on the jaws of your pliers determines the size of your loop.

A

½"

B

C

WIRE WRAPPING

This technique can be used with precious metal and other wires or with headpins and eyepins. It forms a stronger loop and adds a space between the loop and the bead. This is a technique that you need to practice many times to master. To create a small wire wrapped loop at each end of a bead:

1. Cut a piece of wire which is the width of the bead plus about 1½" (Illustration A).

2. With round-nosed pliers, grip the wire about ¾" from the end. Bend the wire around the pliers until a loop is formed and the tail of the wire is perpendicular to the stem (Illustration B).

3. With your fingernail behind the loop, use the pliers to roll it back until it is centered above the stem of the wire (Illustration C).

4. Using your finger or fingernail, wrap the tail of the wire around the stem a couple of turns. Use flat-nosed pliers to finish wrapping the tail tightly. If there is any excess wire, snip it off (Illustrations D and E).

5. Place a bead on the wire. Grip the wire so that the jaws are about ¾" from the bead and roll the pliers until a loop is formed and the tail of the wire is perpendicular to the stem (Illustrations F and B).

6. With your fingernail behind the loop, roll it back until it is centered above the stem of the wire (Illustration C).

7. Using your finger or fingernail, wrap the tail of the wire around the stem a couple of turns, getting tightly between the bead and the loop Use flat-nosed pliers to finish wrapping the tail tightly. Snip off any excess wire (Illustrations D, E).

NOTE
When making a single loop on a headpin or eyepin, cut the wire about ¾" above the bead when making a medium-sized loop.

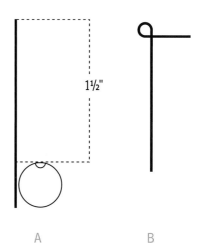

1½"

A   B

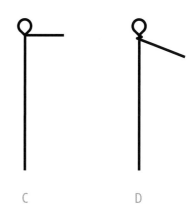

C   D

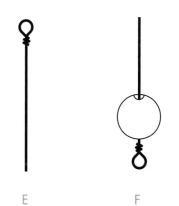

E   F

USING FRENCH WIRE TO ATTACH CLASPS

French wire is a kind of flexible metal sheath that covers part of the silk thread so that it can be attached directly to the clasp.

1. Thread the silk on the needle and knot the end.

2. Thread on 3 pearls and a ¹/₂-inch piece of French wire (Illus. A).

3. Pass the needle through the loop of the clasp and back through the pearl nearest the French wire. Use flat-nosed pliers to pull the needle through first. Then grip the thread just behind the needle and pull the rest of the thread through. As you pull the thread, watch to make sure that the French wire gathers up into a tight loop around the clasp (Illus. B, C).

4. When the pearl lies snugly against both ends of the French wire, make a knot on the other side by forming a loop and passing the needle through. Tighten this knot against the pearl (Illus. D).

5. Now pass the needle the through the next pearl. Slide the pearl tight against the knot you have just made, and make another knot on the other side (Illus. E).

6. Pass the needle the through the last pearl. Slide it tight against the knot you have just made, and make another knot on the other side (Illus. F).

7. Cut away the tail and very end knot of the thread, and put a tiny dab of hypo-cement on the knot you have just made (Illus. G).

8. Finish stringing and knotting all of your pearls until the third pearl from the end. Add the last three pearls to the necklace without putting knots between them (Illus. H).

9. Add ¹¹/₂ inch of French wire, and pass the needle through the loop of the other half of the clasp (llus. I).

TIP

Using French wire requires a little practice and patience. If the holes in the pearls are small, then you should use the thinner size E thread. You can also use a smaller size 6 needle, if necessary.

10. Pass the needle through the loop of the clasp and back through the pearl nearest the French wire. As you pull the thread, watch to make sure that the French wire gathers up into a tight loop around the clasp (llus. J).

11. Make a knot on the other side by forming a loop and passing the needle through. Tighten this knot against the pearl (llus. K).

12. Pass the needle the through the next pearl and make another knot on the other side (llus. L).

13. Pass the needle through the third pearl. Pull the thread very taut, and cut it away as close to the pearl as possible. Use a very sharp-pointed pair of scissors or cutters to get in as close as possible. The ends of the thread should be hidden by the pearl (llus. M).

14. Add a dab of hypo-cement or clear nail polish to the last two knots you made (llus. N).

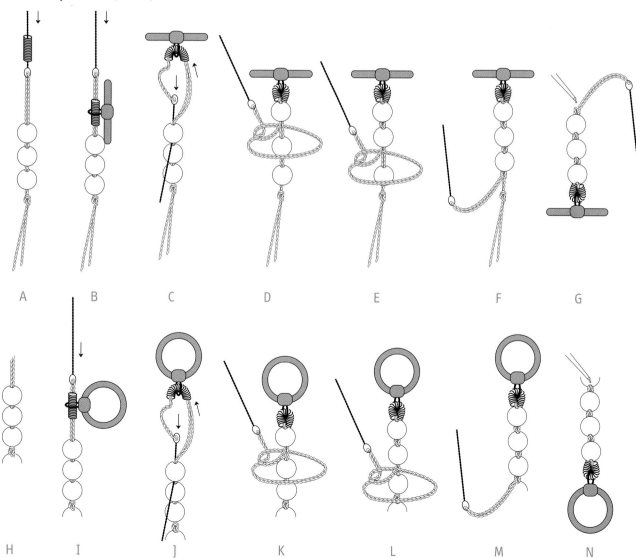

A   B   C   D   E   F   G

H   I   J   K   L   M   N

MAKING A CONTINUOUS STRAND (NO CLASP)

If a necklace is big enough to fit comfortably over your head, it does not need a clasp. This continuous strand method can be used for opera and rope lengths (those measuring at least 30 inches).

1. Double your thread through the needle and tie a knot about six inches from the end. This extra long tail will make it easy for you to grip and tighten the thread as you work.

2. Add three pearls without knotting (Illus. A). Make another knot 2 inches above these pearls (leaving 2 inches of thread empty).

3. Add the rest of your pearls, knotting between each one (Illus. B). Make a knot after the last pearl.

4. Insert your needle into the outside of the very first pearl you started with (that is, the end near the long tail of thread). Pull the needle through and tighten so that all the pearls lie together, with the first three pearls moving up to rest beside the second knot you made (Illus. C).

5. Once the thread is taut and all the pearls are together in a continuous circle, make a knot between the first and second pearl using the loop method described in step 4 on page 24, disregarding the reference to French wire (Illus. D).

6. Pass the needle through the second pearl. Tighten the thread, and make another knot (Illus. E).

7. Pass the needle through the third pearl. Pull the thread very taut, and cut it off as close to the pearl as possible. The tail of the thread should end up hidden in the third pearl. Add a tiny dab of hypo-cement to the knots between the first and second pearls and the second and third pearls (Illus. F).

A   B

C

D

E

F

STANDARD MEASUREMENTS

SIZE

The diameter of beads is commonly described in millimeters. The chart on the following page shows the most common sizes, from 2 to 12 millimeters.

Since beads are often sold in strands measured by the inch, it is useful to know how many beads there are per inch. It is especially useful to know how many comprise a 16-inch strand, a typical length for temporarily strung beads.

LENGTH

One inch = 25.4 millimeters
One foot = 0.3 meters
One millimeter = .04 inches
One meter = 3.3 feet

THICKNESS

Wire thicknesses are measured in American standard gauge or inches or millimeters. The higher the gauge number, the thinner the wire.

Beading wire thicknesses are measured in inches. Note that the last three gauges in the chart to the right are roughly equivalent to the beading wire sizes of .018, .015, and .013.

WEIGHT

If pearls are large, or if they are sold in great quantities, their weight is sometimes expressed in grains, carats, or grams. The grain standard was originally derived from the weight of one grain of barley or wheat, which gives you an idea of its extreme lightness. Ounces can be very confusing in the world of precious metals or gems. The common ounce used in the United States and Britain is an avoirdupois ounce. Precious metals, on the other hand, are weighed in troy ounces, which are about 10 percent heavier.

THICKNESS

The holes in cultured pearls are commonly .6 millimeter in diameter. Wire thicknesses are measured in American standard gauge or inches or millimeters. Note that the higher the gauge number, the thinner the wire.

Beading wire thicknesses are measured in inches. Note that the last three gauges are roughly equivalent to the beading wire sizes of .018, .015, and .013.

Seed beads, however, are a strange exception to the sensible practice of sizing in millimeters. They are, instead, classified by an arcane system that seems to have originated in the nineteenth century in the Czech city of Gablonz. Despite the fact that it is neither very useful nor very consistent, the system has persisted. The reference point starts with a medium-sized glass bead, which has a value of zero. A bead somewhat smaller would have two zeros; one smaller yet, three zeros, and so on. Because very tiny beads have many zeros, it is easier to write them as a number like so: 11/0, meaning the bead is eleven zeros, or eleven sizes smaller than the "zero" reference bead. What makes this system awkward is that the beads with the higher numbers are smaller than the beads with the smaller ones; thus, a 13/0 seed bead is much smaller than an 8/0 seed bead. The situation is even more confusing because Czech standards and Japanese standards vary slightly—the size refers only to the diameter of the bead, not to the width. Keeping in mind that there are differences between different manufacturers' standards, as well as that the widths of individual seed beads often vary, the chart shown on the right can be used as a rough guide to their sizes.

NECKLACE LENGTHS

One of the pleasures of creating your own jewelry is that you can adjust the length of your necklaces so they fit you. A comfortable choker on some necks is a genuine strangler on others, and a centerpiece that is well presented on the faint décolletage of a fashion model might be entirely lost on those who are more generously endowed. If the jewelry is for yourself, disregard the standard lengths and try it on for size as you are making it.

APPROXIMATE BEADS PER INCH:

		1"	7"	16"	18"
Bead Size	2mm	12	88	200	225
	3mm	8	59	134	150
	4mm	6	44	100	114
	5mm	5	35	80	90
	6mm	4	29	67	76
	7mm	3.5	25	58	65
	8mm	3	22	50	57
	9mm	2.5	19	45	40
	10mm	2.5	17	40	45
	12mm	2	14	33	38

		Approximate diameter in millimeters	Approximate number of beads in an inch
Seed bead size	15/0	1.4 to 1.5	32 to 35
	13/0	1.6 to 1.7	24 to 27
	11/0	2.0 to 2.1	18 to 19
	8/0	3.0 to 3.1	11 to 12
	6/0	4.0	8 to 9

WEIGHT CONVERSIONS

1 grain = .0648 grams

1 carat = 0.2 grams

1 gram = 5 carats = .03527 ounces = 15.43 grains

1 avoirdupois ounce = 28.35 grams = 437.5 grains

1 troy ounce = 31.1 grams = 480 grains = 1.097 avoirdupois ounces

WIRE THICKNESS

18-gauge = .0403 inches = 1.02 mm

20-gauge = .0320 inches = 0.81 mm

22-gauge = .0253 inches = 0.64 mm

24-gauge = .0201 inches = 0.51 mm

26-gauge = .0159 inches = 0.40 mm

28-gauge = .0126 inches = 0.32 mm

GETTING THE LENGTH RIGHT

Although you can lay out all your beads in a line and measure them, or place them in the channels of a marked beading board, there is really only one sure way of getting the length right. Just before you think you are halfway through stringing the beads, hold the uncompleted necklace with the clasp at the back of your neck. Looking in a mirror, you can then judge exactly where the strand will fall. This step is critical in any necklace with a centerpiece or a centered pattern, but it is something I do with every single necklace I am making for myself.

THE "STANDARDS"

Although you will decide the right lengths for your own body, it is useful for jewelry makers to have a general reference guide. There are a variety of opinions about terminology and standard lengths. One woman's "long opera" is another's "rope." The following is as good a guide as any, but remember that the best standard lengths are those you create for yourself. Since a bracelet is, to the maker, just a very short necklace, we start with that length.

Bracelet	7 to 8 inches
Choker	13 to 15 inches
Standard short	16 to 17 inches
Standard long	18 to 20 inches
Matinee	About 24 inches
Opera	30 to 40 inches
Rope	40 inches and longer

CLASP LENGTH

A 16-inch strand of beads, knotted with a fish hook clasp will be about 18 inches long when it's finished. If 18 inches isn't long enough, add a few sterling or gold-filled round beads before the clasp. Or if you are using a hook clasp, add some chain to your bead tip on the opposite side to the hook.

BRACELETS

DICHROIC GLASS BRACELET

DICHROIC GLASS BEADS CAN BE EXPENSIVE, BUT JUST A DOZEN OR SO CAN MAKE A MEMORABLE BRACELET. WHILE NEARLY ALL OF THESE BEADS DIFFER IN SHAPE OR PATTERN, THEY ARE NONETHELESS UNITED BY THEIR RED TONES (RED CALLS FOR GOLD). IN THIS CASE, I USED A MORE ECONOMICAL VERMEIL. THIS KIND OF RANDOM DESIGN IS GREAT FOR USING UP LEFTOVER BEADS FROM OTHER PROJECTS.

1. First, make the dangle which will hang on the clasp. Onto the headpin add a 3mm gold bead, a dichroic glass bead, and another 3mm gold bead. Use the round-nosed pliers to begin a wire-wrapped loop with the rest of the headpin. Slip the loop over the ring of the circular part of the toggle clasp and close it by wire wrapping.

2. Thread a crimp onto the beading wire. Pass the beading wire through the ring of the same half of the clasp and then back through the crimp. Make sure the beading wire is tight around the ring. Squeeze the crimp shut. Thread on a 3mm gold bead and a small dichroic bead. Continue to add combinations of dichroic and gold until they are all on the wire. Use the 3mm gold beads as spacers against the large holes of the dichroic beads. This will prevent the beads from sitting loosely on the beading wire.

3. Now, hold the bracelet around your wrist to see if you like how the beads are arranged. Until you are familiar with making this kind of seemingly random selection, it is unlikely that the first arrangement will be the one you want. Luckily, the beads should be easy to remove and rearrange.

4. When the design pleases you and the bracelet fits well, add a 3mm gold bead and a crimp. Bring the beading wire through the ring of the other side of the clasp and then back through the crimp and round bead. Tighten the bracelet so there are no spaces between the beads, close the crimp, and snip off any remaining beading wire. Add the crimp covers.

TOOLS
Wire Cutters, Crimping Pliers, Round-Nosed Pliers

MATERIALS (FOR A 7" BRACELET)
- 12 dichroic glass beads from 5mm round to 18mm x 10mm barrel
- 10 assorted vermeil beads and spacers from 6mm to 12mm
- 18 3mm gold-filled hollow seamless round beads
- 1 13mm vermeil toggle clasp
- 2 gold-filled crimp beads
- 2 gold-filled crimp bead covers
- 1 1" gold-filled headpin with ball end
- 10" of beading wire

HOLLOW SILVER BRACELET

VARY THIS WITH GEMSTONES, SILVER OR GOLD ROUND BEADS.

1. Start by threading on a crimp. Pass the wire through the ring of half of the clasp back through the crimp. Tighten the beading wire around the ring and squeeze the crimp shut.

2. Thread on a black onyx followed by a disc bead. Repeat this pattern 11 times or until the bracelet fits. (Try it around your wrist.)

3. Bring the beading wire through the ring of the other side of the clasp and back through the crimp and round bead. Now tighten the bracelet so there are no spaces between the beads, close the crimp and snip off any remaining beading wire.

TOOLS

Wire Cutters, Crimping Pliers

MATERIALS

12	11 by 5mm hollow silver disc shape beads
13	3mm black onyx round beads
1	silver pendulum clasp
24	silver crimp beads
2	crimp bead covers
10"	of beading wire

SOLID SILVER BRACELET

THIS IS A GREAT WAY TO USE LOVELY AND UNUSUALLY SHAPED BEADS. THE BEADS ARE LIKE LITTLE COFFEE BEANS WITH A PATTERN ON EACH END. FIT THEM SNUGLY IN PAIRS AND THEY CREATE A SOLID ROPE AROUND THE WRIST FULL OF TEXTURE AND REFLECTION. BECAUSE THE BEADS ARE SOLID SILVER AND TIGHTLY PACKED TOGETHER, THE DESIGN IS A BIT TOO HEAVY FOR A NECKLACE, BUT IT LOOKS AND FEELS WONDERFUL AS A BRACE-LET FOR OCCASIONS THAT DEMAND A POWERFUL STATEMENT.

1. Start the bracelet by threading on a crimp. Pass the beading wire through the ring of one half of the clasp back through the crimp. Make sure that the beading wire is tight around the ring and squeeze the crimp shut. Add a crimp cover.

2. Thread on a bean bead so that the concave, or inside, of the bean curves around the crimp cover and hides the tail of the beading wire. Add another bean so that its back is against the back of the

TOOLS

Wire Cutters, Crimping Pliers,

Round-Nosed Pliers

MATERIALS

2	silver crimp beads
10"	of beading wire
1	silver toggle clasp
2	silver crimp covers
39	5mm by 10mm solid silver "bean"-shaped beads
3	2.5mm hollow silver seamless round beads
1	1" silver headpin with ball tip

NOTE

Attaching a dangle to the clasp of a bracelet is not just a decorative feature. The weight of the dangle helps to ensure that the clasp of the bracelet will fall on the underside of your wrist

PROJECT CONTINUED ON PAGE 34

first. Now add another so that the concave side fits snugly into the concave side of the second bean bead. Repeat this pattern of pairs of bean beads seventeen times or until the bracelet is the length you wish.

3. Add a final 2.5mm round bead and a crimp. Bring the beading wire through the ring of the other side of the clasp and back through the crimp and round bead. Tighten the bracelet so there are no spaces between the beads, then close the crimp and snip off any

remaining beading wire. Add the remaining crimp cover.

4. To make the dangle, use the headpin and add a round bead, a pair of bean beads, and another round bead. Use your round-nosed pliers to grip the headpin about ¼" above the bead. Make a loop, attach it to the ring of the clasp, and wrap the tail of the headpin between the bottom of the loop and the top of the bead. (See "Wire-Wrapping" in Jewelry Techniques, page 23.)

PEARL "BERRIES" BRACELET

THE FANCIFUL NAME OF THIS DESIGN COMES FROM ITS MANY DANGLING PIECES, WHICH LOOK A LITTLE LIKE BERRIES ON A VINE. THE TECHNIQUE FOR MAKING THE BERRIES MAY SEEM HARD AT FIRST, BUT IS ACTUALLY QUITE SIMPLE ONCE YOU GET THE HANG OF IT, AND IT CAN BE USED FOR OTHER DESIGNS.

1. To make the berries, start by adding a round bead to a headpin. Then add a bead cap with the concave side facing up. Add 1 pearl. Add another bead cap, this time with the concave side facing down. Add another round bead. Use your round-nosed pliers to grip the headpin about ¼ inch above the bead. Make a loop and wrap the tail of the head pin between the bottom of the loop and the top of the bead (see "Using Headpins and Eyepins," page 22).

2. When you have made all the berries, use a split ring to attach the lobster clasp to the flat cable chain.

3. Open a jump ring. Slip on 3 pearl berries in different colors. Attach the jump ring with the "berry cluster" to the second link down from the clasp. Close it around the link. (See "Using Jump Rings and Split Rings," page 15.)

TOOLS
Wire Cutters, Round-Nosed Pliers, Flat-Nosed Pliers

MATERIALS
52 5.5mm freshwater potato-shaped pearls, in various natural and dyed colors (about three-quarters of a 16" multicolor strand)
52 1" 24-gauge gold-filled headpins
104 2.5mm gold-filled round beads
104 5mm gold-filled bead caps
14 5mm oval gold-filled jump rings
7 ½" gold-filled cable chain with 8mm links
1 11mm gold-filled lobster clasp
1 5mm gold-filled split ring

NOTE
The clasp of this bracelet can be attached to whichever link offers the best fit. If you have a narrow wrist, use the link closest to the last bead, then a cluster or two can dangle down from the clasp.

4. Make another berry cluster (as explained in step 3) and attach it to the chain two links down from the first cluster. You must be very careful to attach all the clusters to the same side of the chain. Hold the chain straight after you add a cluster to make sure it's hanging on the same side as the first. Now make and add the rest of the clusters, attaching them to every other link ot the chain and making sure they are on the same side of the link as the rest. Your last cluster should end on the last chain link. If it does not, check to make sure it fits around your wrist, and then snip off any excess links.

GOLD AND CUBIC ZIRCONIA BRACELET

MULTIPLE STRANDS OF TINY BEADS CREATE A WIDE BAND AND
ARE MORE ECONOMICAL THAN USING LARGE GOLD BEADS.

1. Cut the beading wire into three 10" pieces. Divide the daisy
   spacer, round beads, and cubic zirconia beads into three equal
   parts, keeping the ratio of the colors of the CZ roughly even.

2. Put a piece of scotch tape around one end of a piece of the
   beading wire to prevent the beads falling off. Thread one set of
   beads onto the beading wire in a random pattern. Refer to the
   picture if you need guidance on color balance. When you have
   threaded on all the beads (approximately 6¼"), put another piece
   of tape or a clip on the other end to prevent the beads falling off.

3. Do the same with the next two pieces of beading wire, making
   sure that the length of beads on each of them is exactly the same
   as the first. Be sure the beads are all tightly together when you
   are comparing them.

4. Remove the tape. Thread a crimp onto one of the pieces and pass
   it through the top ring of one half of the clasp and back through
   the crimp. Make sure that the beading wire is tight around the
   ring and squeeze the crimp shut.

5. Remove the tape at the other end of the wire, thread on a crimp,
   and attach in the same way to the bottom ring of the other half of
   the clasp. Make sure all the beads are tightly together before closing the crimp. (Note: The two halves of a sliding clasp must be
   facing in opposite direction to fit together properly.)

6. Attach the second strand in the same way to the middle rings of
   the clasp, and then the third to remaining rings. In each case
   make sure the beads are snug and the lengths of the strands are
   roughly even. (It is unlikely that they will be exactly even, but a
   small difference in length will not be noticeable on your wrist.)
   Add the crimp covers.

TOOLS

Wire Cutters, Crimping Pliers, Tape

MATERIALS (7" BRACELET)

30"	of beading wire (preferably gold-plated)
101	4mm vermeil daisy spacer beads
69	2mm vermeil faceted rounds beads
120	3mm by 4mm multi-colored cubic zirconia (CZ) faceted rondel beads (a little less than a 16" strand of multi-colored CZ)
6	gold-filled crimps
1	vermeil 3 ring slide clasp
6	gold-filled crimp covers

SILVER, GOLD, AND JADE BRACELET

BRACELETS ARE OFTEN VIEWED FROM THE SIDE, ESPECIALLY BY THE PERSON WHO IS WEARING THEM. THE LARGE BRUSHED SILVER DISCS PERFORM WONDERFULLY FROM THIS PERSPECTIVE, SHOWING A LARGE AREA OF PRECIOUS METAL AND REFLECTING THE INTENSE GREEN OF THE JADE.

1. Start the bracelet by threading on a crimp. Pass the beading wire through the ring of one half of the clasp and back through the crimp. Make sure that the beading wire is tight around the ring and squeeze the crimp shut. Add a 6mm gold-filled round bead to cover the tail of the beading wire and cut.

2. Thread on a silver disc, a gold-filled 3mm bead, another disc, a jade bead, a disc, a jade bead, a disc, a jade bead, a 3mm round bead, a disc, a 3mm round bead, a disc, a 3mm round bead, a disc, a 3mm round bead, a jade bead, a disc, a jade bead, a disc, a jade bead, a 3mm round bead, a disc, a 3mm round bead, a disc, a 3mm round bead, a disc, a 3mm round bead, a jade bead, a disc, a jade bead, a disc, a 3mm round bead, a disc, and a 6mm round bead.

3. Add the remaining crimp bead and bring the beading wire through the ring of the other side of the clasp and back through the crimp and last silver round bead. Now tighten the bracelet so that all the beads fit snugly against each other. Close the crimp and snip off any remaining beading wire. Add the crimp covers.

4. To make the dangle, add a 3mm gold-filled round bead to the headpin, then a jade bead, a silver disc, and another 3mm gold-filled round bead. Cut the headpin to leave about ⁵/₈" above the last bead. See "Wire Wrapping," page 23 to make a wire-wrapped loop. Start the loop and slip it onto the ring of the clasp. Close the loop and finish wrapping the wire around its base.

TOOLS

Wire Cutters, Crimping Pliers, Round-Nosed Pliers, Flat-Nosed Pliers

MATERIALS (7" BRACELET)

- 2 silver crimp beads
- 12" of .018 beading wire
- 1 silver spring ring clasp
- 2 6mm gold-filled seamless hollow round beads
- 12 3mm gold-filled seamless hollow round beads
- 16 2mm by 12mm brushed silver discs
- 9 12mm green jade beads
- 2 silver crimp covers
- 1 2" silver headpin

PEARL SILVER BRACELET

SURROUNDING THESE PEARLS WITH SILVER BEADS INCREASES THE GEM'S SILVER HUE. LARGE SPACER BEADS MAKE THE PEARLS LOOK ALMOST AS THOUGH THEY ARE SET IN A BAND OF SILVER.

1. First, make the little pendant that will hang beside the bracelet clasp. To the headpin, add 1 pearl, 1 star-shaped silver bead, and 1 round silver bead. Make a small loop to finish it off.

2. Using a crimp bead, attach the beading wire to the tongue end of the clasp. Now add 3 of the 4 millimeter daisy spacers, 1 pearl, and 1 of the star-shaped silver beads. Repeat this pattern until you have used all the pearls or reached a length of about 6½ inches. Check the bracelet around your wrist. If the length fits, add 1 round silver bead, the pendant, and a crimp. If it is too short, repeat the pattern and measure again. When it fits comfortably around the wrist, atttach to the main part of the box clasp, and add the crimp covers.

TOOLS

Wire Cutters, Crimping Pliers, Round-Nose Pliers

MATERIALS

19	6mm near-round freshwater pearls with a silver hue
10	3–7mm star-shaped sterling silver beads
27	4mm sterling silver daisy spacer beads
2	sterling silver crimp beads
2	sterling silver crimp bead covers
2	2.5mm sterling silver round beads
1	sterling silver head pin with a cubic zircon stud
1	box clasp with moonstone inset
12"	beading wire

RUBY AND PEARL BRACELET

THE PURPLE SILK THREAD AND THE PURPLE-RED RUBIES DEEPEN THE PURPLE TONES OF THE LARGE PEARLS IN THIS STUNNING BRACELET.

1. Double the thread, and attach half the clasp using the clamshell bead tip (see "Using Bead Tips to Attach Clasps," page 18). Make a knot after the bead tip, then string on 1 ruby rondel. Make another knot, then string on 1 pearl (see "Getting Knotted," page 16). Continue alternating rubies with pearls, being sure to knot after each one. Periodically check the size around your wrist. When the length fits around it comfortably, finish off by using the bead tip to attach the thread to the other half of the clasp.

TOOLS

Beading Needle, Awl, Flat-Nosed Pliers, Scissors

MATERIALS

11	10mm near-round freshwater pearls with natural purple hue
12	4mm faceted ruby rondels
2	gold-filled clamshell bead tips
1	gold-filled box clasp
3	ft of size F purple silk embroidery thread

TUTTI BUMPS AND DOTS BRACELET

ALTHOUGH NO ONE BEAD IN THIS BRACELET IS THE SAME COLOR AS ANOTHER, THE DESIGN IS NOT SIMPLY RANDOM. THE BEADS HAVE A COMMON PATTERN OF BUMPS OR DOTS. THE BUMPY BEADS ARE OPPOSITE ONE ANOTHER, AS ARE THE DOTTY BEADS. TO ADD EVEN MORE BALANCE, THE DISC-SHAPED CENTER BEAD IS MATCHED BY A SIMILARLY SIZED DISC-SHAPED TOGGLE CLASP ON THE OPPOSITE SIDE. SO EVEN THOUGH THE OVERALL EFFECT IS ONE OF PLAYFUL, RANDOM COLOR, THERE REMAINS AN UNDERLY-ING SYMMETRY.

1. Thread a crimp onto the beading wire. Pass the last ring of the same half of the clasp back through the crimp. Make sure that the beading wire is tight around the ring. Squeeze the crimp shut. Thread on a round silver bead, 3 seed beads , a daisy spacer bead, a round bumpy bead, a daisy bead, 3 seed beads, a daisy bead, a round dotty glass bead, a daisy bead, 3 seed beads, a daisy bead, a glass dichroic bead with a bumpy edge, a daisy bead, 3 seed beads, a daisy bead, a round dotty bead, a daisy bead, 3 seed beads, a daisy bead, a round silver bead, a daisy bead, and the large glass disc bead.

2. Starting at the daisy bead/round silver bead/daisy bead combi-nation, reverse the pattern above to make the other side of the bracelet. As you go, periodically check to make sure each type of bead sits opposite the same type of bead on the other side of the bracelet.

3. Try the bracelet on for size. Add a crimp. Bring the beading wire through the ring of the other side of the clasp and then back through the crimp and round bead. Now, tighten the bracelet so there are no spaces between the beads, close the crimp, and snip off any remaining beading wire. Add the crimp covers.

TOOLS
Wire Cutters, Crimping Pliers

MATERIALS (FOR A 7" BRACELET)

4	11mm round lampwork glass beads with dot pattern
2	12mm flat disc lampwork glass beads with bumpy edges
2	12mm round lampwork glass beads with bumps
1	15mm flat disc lampwork glass bead with dot pattern
30	size 8/0 black seed beads
18	4mm silver daisy spacer beads
4	3mm silver hollow seamless round beads
1	14mm silver toggle clasp with large decorated rim
2	silver crimp beads
2	silver crimp bead covers
10"	of beading wire

MOSS AQUAMARINE BRACELET

MOSS AQUAMARINE, OR "AQUA" FOR SHORT, IS REALLY JUST A PRETTY TRADE NAME FOR A QUALITY OF AQUAMARINE THAT HAS A LOT OF INCLUSIONS. ALTHOUGH LACK OF CLARITY GREATLY REDUCES THE PRICE OF AQUAMARINE, IT DOES NOT NECESSARILY LESSEN ITS ATTRACTIVENESS, AND IT CAN MAKE LARGER STONES QUITE AFFORDABLE. THE CLOUDY NATURE AND SUBTLE COLORS OF THESE FACETED NUGGETS MAKES THEM IDEAL CANDIDATES FOR JEWELRY OF UNDERSTATED ELEGANCE.

1. Start the bracelet by threading on a crimp. Pass the beading wire through the ring of one half of the clasp and back through the crimp. Make sure that the beading wire is tight around the ring and squeeze the crimp shut.

2. Thread on a 3mm round silver bead and a Thai silver chip so that they fit over the tail of the wire and cut away any excess.

3. Add a moss aqua nugget, a 2.5mm silver round, a Thai silver chip, and another 2.5mm silver round. Repeat this step 8 more times.

4. Add a Thai silver chip, a 3mm round bead, and a crimp. Bring the beading wire through the ring of the other side of the clasp and back through the crimp and the round bead. Tighten the bracelet so that there are no spaces between the beads, close the crimp, and snip off any remaining wire. Add the crimp covers.

5. Make the dangle by adding to the headpin a Thai silver chip, a 2.5mm silver round bead, a moss aqua nugget, a silver round, another Thai silver chip, and the last 2.5mm silver round. Cut the headpin ⁵/₈" above the last bead and start a wrapped loop. Attach it to the loop of the clasp ring and finish it off with several turns around the base.

TOOLS
Crimping Pliers, Flat-Nosed Pliers, Wire Cutters, Round-Nosed Pliers

MATERIALS

10	12mm by 10mm (approximately) faceted moss aquamarine nuggets
12	1mm by 4mm (approximately) Thai silver chips
20	2.5mm hollow silver round beads
2	3mm hollow silver round beads
1	2" silver headpin with ball tip
2	silver crimp beads
2	silver crimp bead covers
1	silver toggle clasp
10"	of beading wire

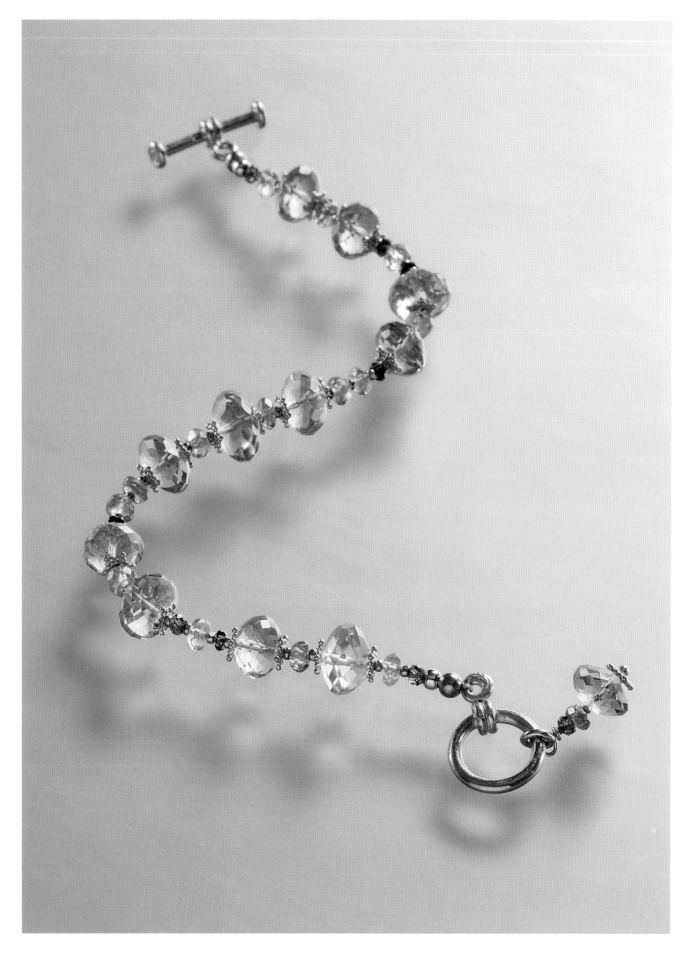

CITRINE BRACELET

THE NATURAL COLOR OF CITRINE IS, AS THE NAME IMPLIES, LEMON YELLOW—AN ALMOST IMPOSSIBLE TONE FOR MANY WOMEN TO WEAR. BUT MOST CITRINE NOW ON THE MARKET IS IN ITS HEAT-TREATED FORM. THIS ENHANCEMENT ADDS A REDEEMING TINGE OF RED (MOST MODERN CITRINE IS ACTUALLY HEAT-TREATED AMETHYST, ANOTHER SILICON DIOXIDE QUARTZ THAT ADAPTS EASILY TO THE PREFERRED COLOR). ALTHOUGH HEAT TREATING GIVES CITRINE A LOVELY WARM GLOW, IT STILL HAS A DANGEROUS TENDENCY TOWARD ORANGE, SO I ALWAYS COMBINE IT WITH MORE MUTED COLORS TO SOFTEN THE EFFECT.

1. Start the bracelet by threading on a crimp. Pass the beading wire through the ring of one half of the clasp and back through the crimp. Make sure that the beading wire is tight around the ring and squeeze the crimp shut.

2. Thread on a 2.5mm round gold round bead so that it fits over the tail of the wire and cut away any excess.

3. Referring to the bead codes in the materials list, add beads as follows: G, C, P, C, D, A, D, C, Z, C, D, A, D, C, G, C, P, C, G, C, D, A, D, C, Z, C, D, A, D, C, G, C, P, C, Z, C, D, A, D, C, Z, D, A.

4. Reverse the order in step 3, beginning with D, to create the other half of the bracelet. Add the other 2.5mm gold bead and a crimp. Bring the beading wire through the ring of the other side of the clasp and back through the crimp and the round beads. Tighten the bracelet so that there are no spaces between the beads, close the crimp, and snip off any remaining wire. Add the crimp covers.

5. Make the dangle by adding a gold daisy, citrine, charlotte, zircon, garnet, and another charlotte to the headpin. Form the rest of the headpin into a wire-wrapped loop. Use the jump ring to attach the dangle to the ring of the clasp.

TOOLS
Crimping Pliers, Flat-Nosed Pliers, Wire Cutters, Round-Nosed Pliers

MATERIALS

12	5mm by 8mm faceted citrine rondel beads (A)
9	2mm by 4mm faceted natural zircon rondel beads (Z)
6	2mm by 4mm faceted peridot rondel beads (P)
9	3mm faceted garnet round beads (G)
23	4mm vermeil star daisy spacer beads (D)
32	size 15/0 gold-plated charlotte beads (C)
2	2.5mm hollow gold-filled round beads
1	4mm gold-filled jump ring
1	1¼" gold-filled headpin with ball tip
2	gold-filled crimp beads
2	gold-filled crimp bead covers
1	vermeil toggle clasp
10"	of beading wire

NOTE
If there is any size variation in the citrine beads, reserve the largest for the central bead of the bracelet.

LABRADORITE ON CHAIN BRACELET

CHAIN CAN BE USED EITHER AS A MAJOR AESTHETIC ELEMENT OF A BRACELET OR SIMPLY AS THE STRUCTURAL FRAMEWORK. THESE FACETED LABRADORITE NUGGETS ARE SO DELIGHTFUL THAT I WANTED THEIR SHIMMERING IRIDESCENCE TO DOMINATE THE DESIGN, LETTING THE CHAIN SLIP INTO THE BACKGROUND. SILVER GOES SO WELL WITH LABRADORITE, HOWEVER, THAT I DID NOT WANT ITS INFLUENCE TO BE COMPLETELY LOST, AND I ADDED A FEW SILVER GRANULATED BEADS TO RESTORE BALANCE AND PROVIDE SOME CONTRASTING TEXTURE.

1. Begin by making the dangles. Add either a labradorite or a granulated silver bead and then a 1.5mm silver bead onto each headpin. If necessary, cut the headpin about $5/8$" above the last bead and make a wire-wrapped loop.

2. Use the jump rings to attach the dangles and the clasp to the links of the chain. Start at the first link and attach the bar part of the toggle clasp using two jump rings to hold it securely. Reserve one labradorite and one silver dangle for the "tail" of the bracelet. Leaving 1 link empty, start adding the dangles to every link of the chain. The silver dangles should be placed at odd intervals between the labradorite. I have used 2 labradorite (L), then a silver (S), 5L, S, 5L, S, 5L, S, 6L, S, 5L. When you have added all the dangles (except the 2 reserved), use 2 jump rings to attach the next link to the other half of the clasp.

3. Now add a silver dangle to the last link of the chain and a labradorite dangle to the very last link. This creates the "tail" that hangs below the clasp.

TOOLS
Round-Nosed Pliers, Flat-Nosed Pliers, Wire Cutters

MATERIALS

	$7^1/_2$" of 7 by 5mm hammered silver flat cable chain
29	11mm by 10mm (approximately) faceted labradorite nuggets (L)
6	7mm Bali-style round granulated silver beads (S)
35	1.5mm faceted Thai silver round beads
39	5mm silver jump rings (at least 20 gauge in thickness)
35	$1^1/_4$" silver headpins with ball tips
1	hammered silver toggle clasp

NOTE
When attaching dangles of this size to a chain bracelet, you need to use jump rings that are sufficiently sturdy. If the wire is too thin, there is a risk they will open with wear. Use a reasonably thick jump ring made from 20- or 18-gauge wire. If the bracelet is heavy, constant wear will place a lot of pressure on the jump rings that secure the clasp to the ends of the chain. For extra security, use two jump rings to attach each half of the clasp.

LABRADORITE ON CHAIN BRACELET

GEMS ON A CHAIN BRACELET

THIS DESIGN IS AN EXCELLENT WAY OF USING THE LEFTOVER BEADS FROM PREVIOUS PROJECTS OR TO DISPLAY INDIVIDUAL BEADS THAT YOU FOUND IRRESISTIBLE DURING YOUR LATEST BEAD SHOPPING EXPEDITION. THE MATERIALS LIST SHOWS THE GEMSTONES I HAVE USED, BUT AS IN A CHARM BRACELET, YOU WILL WANT TO USE YOUR OWN SELECTION OF BEADS.

1. Begin by making the dangles. Slip a gemstone bead onto a headpin and choose something of suitable size and design to go with it from your assortment of silver beads. The greater the assortment of silver beads you have nearby, the greater your choice. If the hole of the gemstone bead is bigger than the ball of the headpin, start with a silver bead. Once the little dangle pleases you, cut the headpin about 1/2" above the last bead and make a wire-wrapped loop.

2. Use the jump rings to attach the dangles and the clasp to the links of the chain. Start at the first link and add 2 dangles. Go to the 4th link and add the spring ring part of the clasp. Note: This will form a "tail" on the bracelet that hangs below the clasped part. This is not just a decorative part of the design, but also a practical one. The weight of this tail helps keep the clasped part of the bracelet hanging underneath your wrist so that you don't have to constantly worry that the bracelet is presenting itself properly.

3. Add a dangle on every second link, making sure as you go that they are all on the same side of the chain. Hold up the chain and stretch it out to see that they are hanging consistently. When you have used all your dangles or the bracelet is long enough, cut off any excess links and add the other half of the clasp to the last link.

TOOLS
Round-Nosed Pliers, Flat-Nosed Pliers, Wire Cutters

MATERIALS

7" of 7mm by 5mm silver flat cable chain

19 assorted gemstone beads (Pictured are 3 keishi pearls, 3 blue agate, 2 kyanite coins, 2 tourmaline rectangles, 1 carved lapis lazuli, 2 chrysoprase, 1 blue topaz oval, 1 peridot and amethyst, 1 turquoise set in silver flower, 2 amethyst drops, 1 apatite with opal)

29 assorted silver beads (Pictured are seventeen 2mm hollow round beads, three 4mm hollow round beads, 5 Thai silver chips, 3 bead caps, 1 silver dangle, four 4mm daisy spacer beads)

21 5mm silver jump rings

19 1 1/4" silver headpins with ball tips

1 8mm silver spring ring clasp

LAMPWORK AND PRESSED GLASS BRACELET

DISC-SHAPED BEADS ARE OFTEN IDEAL FOR BRACELETS. THEY CREATE A BROAD BAND OF COLOR AROUND THE WRIST AND LAY FLATTER AND MORE COMFORTABLY THAN A SIMILAR-SIZED ROUND BEAD.

1. First, make the little dangle that will hang beside the clasp. Add a 3mm silver bead, a 6mm glass bead, and another silver 3mm bead to the headpin. Use the round-nosed pliers to make a loop at the top of the headpin, but do not close it completely. Slip the loop over the ring of the circular part of the toggle clasp and close it by wire-wrapping.

2. Thread a crimp onto the beading wire. Pass the beading wire through the ring of the same half of the clasp and then back through the crimp. Make sure the beading wire is tight around the ring. Squeeze the crimp shut. Thread on a silver bead, a disc bead, another silver bead, and a round glass bead. Repeat this pattern six times.

3. Try the bracelet on for size. Add a crimp. Bring the beading wire through the ring of the other side of the clasp and back through the crimp and the round bead. Now tighten the bracelet so there are no spaces between the beads, close the crimp, and snip off any remaining beading wire. Add the crimp covers.

TOOLS

Wire Cutters, Crimping Pliers, Round-Nosed Pliers, Flat-Nosed Pliers

MATERIALS (FOR A 7" BRACELET)

7	15mm disc lampwork glass beads
8	6mm round lampwork glass beads
17	3mm silver hollow seamless round beads
1	16mm silver toggle clasp
2	silver crimp beads
2	silver crimp bead covers
1	1" silver headpin with ball end
10"	of silver beading wire

TRIANGLE LAMPWORK BEAD BRACELET

TRIANGULAR BEADS CAN BE USED VERY EFFECTIVELY IN BRACELETS. ONE OF THE FLAT SURFACES SITS VERY COMFORTABLY AGAINST THE WRIST, WHILE THE APEX OF THE TRIANGLE FORMS A PROMINENT PYRAMID. THE VIBRANT, CONTEMPORARY COLORS OF THESE BOHEMIAN LAMPWORK BEADS, DESIGNED BY ALENA CHLADKOVA, ATTRACT IMMEDIATE ATTENTION.

1. Thread a crimp onto the beading wire. Pass the wire through the ring of the same half of the clasp and then back through the crimp. Make sure that the beading wire is tight around the ring. Squeeze the crimp shut. Thread on a silver daisy spacer bead, a 4mm round glass bead, another silver daisy, and an opaque triangle bead. Repeat this pattern 6 more times, but make the second, fourth, and sixth triangle beads transparent ones.

2. Try the bracelet around your wrist for size. Add a silver daisy, a round bead, another daisy, and a crimp. Bring the beading wire through the ring of the other side of the clasp and then back through the crimp and the round bead. Now, tighten the bracelet so there are no spaces between the beads, close the crimp, and snip off any remaining beading wire. Add the crimp covers.

TOOLS
Wire Cutters, Crimping Pliers

MATERIALS (FOR AN 8" BRACELET)

- 4   16mm x 14mm triangular lampwork glass beads in an opaque base color
- 3   16mm x 14mm triangular lampwork glass beads in a transparent base color
- 8   6mm round pressed glass beads
- 16   4mm silver daisy spacer beads
- 1   16mm silver toggle clasp
- 2   silver crimp beads
- 2   silver crimp bead covers
- 10"   of beading wire

PEARL AND MARCASITE BRACELET

UNLIKE A TWO-STRAND NECKLACE, THE STRANDS OF THIS SEVEN-INCH BRACELET NEED TO BE ROUGHLY THE SAME LENGTH TO FORM PARALLEL ROWS AROUND YOUR WRIST.

1. Cut the beading wire into two 10-inch lengths, and use the crimp to attach one piece to the top loop of the clasp. String on a pearl and a rondel. Repeat this until you have strung 29 pearls. Make sure the pearls and rondels all fit snugly together. Try the bracelet around your wrist. If it is the right size, add the crimp and attach the strand to the other half of the clasp, taking care to attach it to the appropriate loop.

2. Make a second strand in the same way as the first and attach it to the remaining loops of the clasp.

TOOLS

Wire Cutters, Crimping Pliers

MATERIALS

- 42   7.5mm silver-gray freshwater pearls with a light purple hue (about ³/₄ of a 16" strand)
- 40   6mm Thai silver-and-marcasite rondels
- 4   silver crimp beads
- 4   sterling silver crimp bead covers
- 1   sterling silver 2-loop sliding clasp
- 20"   beading wire

NOTE

Because of the variation in pearl sizes, one strand of the bracelet will probably end up being a little longer than the other. Your wrist is not a perfect cylinder, so if you wear the bracelet the right way around, this difference in length will fit into the wrist's natural contours.

LAZY DAISY BRACELET

1. Attach a piece of tape to one end of the elastic so that the beads do not fall off. Then string on one gold-filled bead and nine silver daisy beads. Repeat this pattern eight times.

2. Take the two loose ends of the elastic cord and make an overhand knot. Tighten it so that all the beads are firmly together. There should not be any spaces between the beads, but do not over tighten. Make a second overhand knot on top of the first, being careful not to allow the cord to slacken and create any gaps. Apply a drop of clear nail polish to the knot. Once the knot is dry, tuck it inside the hole of the gold bead to hide it.

TOOLS

Clear Nail Polish, Scotch tape

MATERIALS

10" of .08 clear elastic beading cord

9   7mm gold-filled seamless hollow round beads

81   4mm silver daisy spacer beads

GOLD AND HANDMADE GLASS BRACELET

ALTHOUGH "GEMSTONE" SOUNDS BETTER THAN "GLASS," THE REALITY IS THAT SOME GLASS BEADS ARE NOT ONLY MORE FASCINATING THAN SOME GEMSTONES BUT ALSO MORE EXPENSIVE. THE DELICATE SWIRL PATTERN AND PINK HUE OF THESE BOHEMIAN LAMPWORK GLASS BEADS CRY OUT TO BE ACCOMPANIED BY GOLD—OR AT LEAST VERMEIL AND GOLD-FILLED BEADS!

1. Start the bracelet by threading on a crimp. Pass the beading wire through the ring of one half of the clasp and back through the crimp. Make sure that the beading wire is tight around the ring and squeeze the crimp shut. Add a 3mm gold-filled round bead to cover the tail of the beading wire and cut.

2. Thread on three vermeil chips, a gold-filled round, a glass bead, and another gold-filled round. Repeat this pattern another seven times. Add three more chips and a gold-filled round.

3. Add the remaining crimp bead and bring the beading wire through the ring of the other side of the clasp and back through the crimp and last gf round bead. Tighten the bracelet so that all the beads fit snugly against each other. Close the crimp and snip off any remaining beading wire. Add the crimp covers.

4. To make the dangle, add a 3mm gold-filled bead to the head-pin, then a glass bead, another 3mm gold-filled bead, and 3 vermeil chips. Cut the headpin to leave about ⅝" above the last bead. See Jewelry Techniques to make a wire-wrapped loop. Start the loop and slip it onto the beading wire between the crimp cover and the adjacent round bead. Close the loop and finish wrapping the wire around its base.

TOOLS
Crimping Pliers, Wire Cutters, Round-Nosed Pliers, Flat-Nosed Pliers

MATERIALS (7" BRACELET)
2   gold-filled crimp beads
1' of beading wire
1   vermeil hook-and-eye clasp
20 3mm gold-filled seamless hollow round beads
30 3mm to 4mm vermeil (or Thai silver) "chip" spacer beads
9   11mm Bohemian lampwork glass pink beads
2   gold-filled crimp covers
1   1½" vermeil headpin with ball tip

NECKLACES

GOLD AND CORAL NECKLACE

(PICTURED ON OPPOSING PAGE, TOP)

GOLD AND CORAL GO TOGETHER BEAUTIFULLY, BUT THERE ARE
SERIOUS QUESTIONS ABOUT THE SUSTAINABILITY AND ECOLOGI-
CAL IMPACT OF GEM-QUALITY CORAL GATHERING. THE CORAL
USED IN THIS PIECE IS FROM AN OLD NECKLACE. IF YOU HAVE
TROUBLE FINDING CORAL BEADS OR DON'T WISH TO ENCOURAGE
NEW PRODUCTION, SMALL RUBY BEADS WOULD DO JUST AS
NICELY.

1. Start the necklace by threading on a crimp. Pass the beading
    wire through the ring of one half of the clasp back through the
    crimp. Make sure that the beading wire is tight around the ring
    and squeeze the crimp shut. Cut off the tail of the wire very close
    to the crimp.

2. Thread on twenty-nine coral beads, then a gold bead and a coral
    bead. Repeat this coral and gold bead pattern another forty-two
    times. Try the necklace around your neck for size and add or
    subtract beads as necessary.

3. Add a final gold bead and the remaining twenty-nine coral
    beads. Bring the beading wire through the ring of the other side
    of the clasp and back through the crimp. Now tighten the
    necklace so that all the beads fit snugly. Close the crimp and snip
    off any remaining beading wire close to the crimp. Add the crimp
    covers.

TOOLS

Wire Cutters, Crimping Pliers

MATERIALS

2	gold-filled crimp beads
20"	of .013 beading wire (The holes in the coral beads are very small.)
1	18 karat gold hook-and-eye clasp
100	2mm round coral beads
44	4.5mm by 6.5mm 18 karat gold side-drilled oblong beads
2	gold-filled crimp covers

COLORS OF ANCIENT EGYPT NECKLACE

(PICTURED ON PAGE 60, BOTTOM)

MANY YEARS AGO I HAD THE GOOD FORTUNE TO VISIT TO THE EGYPTIAN MUSEUM IN CAIRO. I WAS AMAZED TO SEE 3,000-YEAR-OLD JEWELRY LOOKING AS IF IT COULD BE TAKEN FROM THE CASE AND WORN TO A SOPHISTICATED PARTY IN NEW YORK. THAT THE MATERIALS LOOKED FRESH DID NOT SURPRISE ME, FOR THEY WERE ALL TIMELESS GOLD AND GEMSTONES. BUT THE ENTIRELY "MODERN" SENSE OF COLOR WAS UNEXPECTED AND GAVE ME A FEELING OF EMPATHY WITH THESE ANCIENT DESIGNERS.

1. Thread on a crimp. Pass the beading wire through the ring of one half of the clasp back through the crimp. Be sure that the wire is tight around the ring and squeeze the crimp shut. Add a 2mm gold round bead to cover the tail of the wire and cut.

2. Because this asymmetrical necklace has a random order, refer to the picture for guidance threading on the beads, or create your own arrangement. It is important, however, that the five turquoise beads at the bottom are placed symmetrically and the three top-drilled turquoise beads are separated equally. In order to achieve this, check the length around your neck when you have reached 9". If it seems that another ½" will bring the necklace to the desired center point on your neck, add one of the smaller top-drilled beads, a 2mm round bead, a daisy spacer bead, another 2mm round bead, then the largest of the top-drilled beads, 2mm round bead, daisy spacer bead, 2mm round bead, and then the last of the top-drilled beads. Now add several gemstone and spacer beads until they are equal to the length of beads, separating the last turquoise bead from the first top-drilled bead. At that point add a turquoise bead and continue the random design with the rest of the beads, making sure that you reserve at least three smaller beads for the very end of the necklace.

3. Add the remaining crimp bead and bring the beading wire through the ring of the other side of the clasp and back through the crimp and last two or three beads. Tighten the necklace so that all the beads fit snugly against each other. Close the crimp and snip off any remaining beading wire. Add the crimp covers.

TOOLS

Wire Cutters, Crimping Pliers

MATERIALS

- 2 gold-filled crimp beads
- 20" of gold-plated beading wire
- 1 18 karat gold toggle clasp
- 25 2mm 18 karat gold seamless hollow round beads
- 12 turquoise faceted nuggets approximately 10mm by 8mm
- 3 turquoise top-drilled faceted nuggets between 13mm and 17mm in length
- 35 3mm 18 karat gold daisy spacer beads
- 33 2mm by 2.5mm purple garnet faceted rondel beads
- 22 3mm by 4mm spessartine faceted rondel beads
- 18 3mm by 4mm ruby faceted rondel beads
- 13 7mm 18 karat gold faceted seamless hollow round beads with resin cores
- 6 6mm 18 karat gold faceted seamless hollow round beads with resin cores
- 1 3mm coral round bead
- 2 gold-filled crimp covers

HOLLOW GOLD NECKLACE

ALTHOUGH THESE LOVELY HAND-CAST GOLD BEADS ARE COMPLETELY HOLLOW AND VERY LIGHT, THEIR UNEVEN EXTERIOR GIVES AN IMPRESSION OF SOLIDITY. BY MIMICKING THE ROUGH SURFACE OF GOLD NUGGETS, THEY LOOK AS IF THEY WERE SOLID GOLD.

1. Start the necklace by threading on a crimp. Pass the beading wire through the ring of one half of the clasp back through the crimp. Make sure that the beading wire is tight around the ring and squeeze the crimp shut.

2. Now thread on the 60 gold beads. Try the necklace around your neck for size and add or subtract beads as necessary.

3. Bring the beading wire through the ring of the other side of the clasp and back through the crimp and round bead. Now tighten the necklace so that all the beads fit snugly. Close the crimp and snip off any remaining beading wire. Add the crimp covers.

TOOLS

Wire Cutters, Crimping Pliers

MATERIALS

2   gold-filled crimp beads

20" of beading wire

1   18 karat gold toggle clasp

60   6mm by 9mm 18 karat gold hollow rondel beads

2   gold-filled crimp covers

SPACER NECKLACE

THE BEADS IN THIS DESIGN WOULD BE USED AS SPACERS IN OTHER NECKLACES. HERE THEY BALANCE EACH OTHER TO CREATE AN EQUAL PARTNERSHIP.

1. Start the necklace by threading on a crimp. Pass the beading wire through the ring of one half of the clasp back through the crimp. Make sure that the beading wire is tight around the ring and squeeze the crimp shut. Add a silver spacer bead to cover the tail of the beading wire and cut.

2. Thread on a round bead and a spacer bead. Repeat pattern 63 times.

3. Add the remaining crimp and bring the wire through the ring of the other side of the clasp and back through the crimp and last spacer. Tighten so that all the beads fit snugly. Close the crimp and snip off any remaining wire. Add the crimp covers.

TOOLS
Wire Cutters, Crimping Pliers

MATERIALS

  2   silver crimp beads
20" of beading wire
  1   silver ring clasp
64   3mm granulated silver spacer beads
63   4mm seamless hollow silver round beads
  2   silver crimp covers

GOLD WITH SILVER CAPS NECKLACE

USING A BEAD CAP CAN SOMETIMES PRODUCE AN EXCITING NEW LOOK FOR AN ORDINARY BEAD. HERE, THE SILVER CAP FITS SO TIGHTLY AROUND THE PLAIN ROUND GOLD BEAD THAT IT SEEMS AS IF THE SILVER HAS BEEN FUSED TO THE GOLD, FORMING A SINGLE INTRICATE DESIGN.

1. Start the necklace by threading on a crimp. Pass the beading wire through the ring of one half of the clasp back through the crimp. Make sure that the beading wire is tight around the ring and squeeze the crimp shut. Add a gold round bead cover the tail of the beading wire and cut.

2 Now thread on a silver 2.5mm bead and a gold 2.5mm bead, then the gold 4mm bead.

3. Add a silver bead cap, a 9mm gold bead and a 3mm silver bead. Repeat this pattern 33 times but for the last silver round bead use a 4mm bead instead of 3mm. Try the necklace around your neck to make sure it is the correct length.

4. Add the final gold and silver 2.5mm beads. Bring the beading wire through the ring of the other side of the clasp and back through the crimp and round beads. Now tighten the necklace so that all the bead caps fit snugly on the round beads. Close the crimp and snip off any remaining beading wire. Add the final crimp cover.

TOOLS

Wire Cutters, Crimping Pliers

MATERIALS

34	9mm seamless hollow gold-filled round beads
34	10mm silver bead caps
2	2.5mm seamless hollow silver beads
2	2.5mm seamless hollow gold-filled beads
33	43mm seamless hollow silver beads
1	4mm seamless hollow silver bead
1	4mm seamless hollow gold-filled bead
2	silver crimp beads
2	gold-filled crimp covers
1	silver gold toggle clasp
20"	of beading wire

CRYSTAL AND SEED BEAD NECKLACE

1. Cut the beading wire into two 54" pieces and three 26" pieces. To one of the long pieces, add three 2.5mm beads, the loop of the toggle ring, and three more 2.5mm beads on the cone so the beads and toggle loop are sitting inside of it. Now, pass the other long piece of beading wire through the same beads so its ends are even with the first strand. Place the tip of the cone in the center of the beading wire strands. Turn the ends of the wires on the round bead side of the cone into its base and through the tip. Adjust them so the ends of the doubled strands are even. You should now have a loop of round gold beads holding the toggle ring, which should fit neatly inside the cone, with four even lengths of beading wire stretching away from the tip of the cone.

2. Take the three shorter lengths of beading wire and fit their ends through a single large crimp bead. Squeeze the crimp very tight so it grips all three strands at their ends. Pass the free ends of the three strands through the inside of the cone and out the tip. Pull the free ends of the strands to work the crimped end down inside the cone until it is caught at the tip. Adjust the strands on the toggle ring loop, if necessary, so the crimp is hidden by the cone. All the strands should now be held securely inside the cone, with seven lengths of beading wire stretching away from the tip of the cone.

3. Add the charlotte beads, the smaller crystal beads, the daisy beads, and the round gold beads to one of the lengths of beading wire. This pattern is random, but you can use the illustration for reference. When you have beaded between 22" and 24" of the strand or have at least 2" still bare, add one crimp bead and one of the larger crystal beads. Now, add a single charlotte bead and turn the beading wire back through the hole of the large crystal bead and up through the crimp bead. Make sure all the beads fit snugly, close the crimp, and snip off the remaining tail of the wire.

4. Repeat this process for each of the other six strands. As you add beads to a strand, compare it with the ones you have already completed. Stagger the crystal beads so they create a pleasing effect. Make each of the strands a different length between approximately 22" and 24". To wear the necklace, simply put it around your neck and drop the ends of the strands through the toggle ring one at a time.

TOOLS
Wire Cutters, Crimping Pliers, Flat-Nosed Pliers

MATERIALS

7	assorted large crystal beads from 7mm to 10mm
270	smaller crystal beads from 3mm to 6mm
12	12" strands of size 13/0 gold- plated charlotte seed beads
100	2.5mm hollow gold- filled round beads
75	4mm vermeil daisy spacers
1	16mm vermeil ring of a toggle clasp (You do not need the toggle bar.)
1	12mm vermeil cones
20	gold- filled crimp beads
16'	of beading wire

NOTE
I have used two effective methods to fit all seven strands neatly into the cone. To make this work, you must attach the beading wire strands before adding the beads.

VERMEIL, PEARLS, AND AQUAMARINE NECKLACE

THIS KIND OF DESIGN IS AN EXCELLENT WAY TO USE THE LEFTOVER BEADS FROM PREVIOUS PROJECTS OR TO DISPLAY INDIVIDUAL BEADS THAT YOU FOUND IRRESISTIBLE DURING YOUR LATEST BEAD SHOPPING EXPEDITION. MAKE SURE WHEN ADDING THE CHARMS TO ATTACH THEM ALL TO THE SAME SIDE OF THE CHAIN.

1. Start by making the aqua, pearl, and vermeil bead charms ready to dangle off the chain. Use the 2.5mm round beads and the daisy spacer beads to top and tail the dangle, but mix them to make several variations—with a daisy at the bottom and a round at the top, a daisy or a round top and bottom, or even a round and a daisy combination. Refer to the picture for guidance. All the dangles are made using the same technique: Starting with a 2" headpin, add a 2.5mm round or a daisy, or both. Then add one principal bead (aquamarine, vermeil, or pearl). Add the topping daisy or 2.5mm round. To see how they look, you can put all the beads on the headpins and lay them side-by-side before making the loops. That way, you can change any arrangements you don't like. When you are satisfied that all the dangles look good, cut the headpins so that about 5/8" remains above the beads. Use your round-nosed pliers to make a wire-wrapped loop.

2. Lay the charms out in a line and arrange them in a random but balanced manner. Cut a 26" length of chain. Five inches from the beginning of the chain, add your first charm using your 3.5mm gold-filled jump rings. Every other loop, attach a charm.

3. With the leftover 3" length of chain, add one charm hanging from the bottom. On the next loop, add one charm on either side of the chain. Add a charm on the fourth and fifth loops. 4. Add a 3.5mm jump ring to the other end of the 3" chain and attach it to the 6mm heavy gauge jump ring. Attach the same 6mm jump ring to the end of the 26" length of chain and the loop of the lobster clasp. Close all the jump rings.

TOOLS
Round-Nosed Pliers, Flat-Nosed Pliers, Wire Cutters

MATERIALS

11	10mm by 12mm to 25mm by 13mm faceted aqua drops
11	9mm by 9mm potato pearls
17	assorted vermeil and gold-filled charms
q	and seamless hollow round beads
54	2.5mm gold-filled seamless hollow round beads
30	4mm vermeil daisy spacer beads
37	2" vermeil headpins with ball tips
29"	of 7mm by 6mm gold-filled flat cable chain
39	3.5mm gold-filled jump rings
1	6mm 19-gauge gold-filled jump ring
1	22mm vermeil lobster clasp

NOTE
Before starting this necklace, you will need to read how to make a wire-wrapped loop in the Jewelry Techniques section.

VERMEIL AND TOURMALINE NECKLACE

NO MATTER HOW FLEXIBLE BEADING WIRE BECOMES, IT IS DOUBTFUL IT WILL EVER PRECISELY MATCH THE LOOK OF SILK. THE LIGHT WEIGHT OF THESE BEADS DEMANDS A DELICACY THAT ONLY SILK CAN PROVIDE. THE LOVELY VERMEIL BEADS TAKE THE CONCEPT OF HOLLOWNESS TO THE EXTREME-THE PERFORATIONS ADD INTEREST, BUT REDUCE WEIGHT AND THEREFORE COST. THE BEAUTIFUL TOURMALINE STICKS ARE PIECES OF SINGLE CRYSTALS WHOSE GREEN-BLUE COLOR CONTAINS TRACES OF YELLOW, WHICH BLENDS PERFECTLY WITH THE GOLD. USING TURQUOISE-COLORED SILK ENHANCES THE LOOK OF THE GEMS.

1. Read the instructions in Jewelry Techniques for stringing on silk thread and basket bead tips (page 16 and page 20). Note that in this design you are not going to knot between every bead, but between groups of beads as outlined in step 2 below. Start the necklace by threading a beading needle and making a knot at the end of the doubled thread. Following the instructions in "Basket Bead Tips," add one of the basket bead tips.

2. Add five green tourmaline sticks and make a knot. Use your awl to make sure that the knot is tight against the beads. Now add three sticks and knot (always using the awl to make sure that the knots keep the beads tight against each other), another five sticks and knot, another three sticks and knot, and another five sticks and knot.

3. Add a 3mm gold-filled bead, then a 12mm vermeil bead, another 3mm bead, five tourmaline sticks and knot, three sticks and knot, and five sticks and knot. Repeat this pattern eight times.

4. Add five tourmaline sticks and knot, three sticks and knot, five sticks and knot, three sticks and knot, and another five sticks and knot.

5. And one more knot and then the other basket bead tip. Attach the toggle clasp to the bead tips.

TOOLS
Beading Needle, Awl, Scissors, Flat-Nosed Pliers

MATERIALS

2 yards of #83 turquoise silk thread, size F

2 gold-filled basket bead tips

169 green tourmaline sticks approximately 3mm wide and 5mm to 10mm long (A 16" strand will leave enough extra sticks for a pair of earrings)

18 3mm gold-filled seamless hollow round beads

9 12mm vermeil hollow round beads with perforated star pattern

1 vermeil toggle clasp

LONDON BLUE TOPAZ
NECKLACE (PICTURED ON PAGE 74-75)

CLEAR TOPAZ IS COMMONLY TREATED TO PRODUCE STUNNING
SHADES OF BLUE. "LONDON" BLUE IS THE NAME FOR A MEDIUM
TO DARK GRAYISH BLUE SOMETIMES DESCRIBED AS A LITTLE
"INKY". IT IS A RICH AND DIGNIFIED COLOR WHICH GOES PER-
FECTLY WITH GOLD.

1. Start the necklace by threading on a crimp. Pass the beading
    wire through the ring of one half of the clasp back through the
    crimp. Make sure that the beading wire is tight around the ring
    and squeeze the crimp shut.

2. Thread on seven gold beads and a London blue topaz bead.
    Repeat this pattern twenty-one times or until the necklace is the
    length you wish. (Remember to try it around your neck to make
    sure.)

3. Add a final set of seven gold beads and a crimp. Bring the
    beading wire through the ring of the other side of the clasp and
    back through the crimp and round bead. Now tighten the
    necklace so there are no spaces between the beads. Close the
    crimp and snip off any remaining beading wire.

TOOLS

Wire Cutters, Crimping Pliers

MATERIALS

  2 gold-filled micro-crimp beads

20" of .013 beading wire

  1 18 karat gold toggle clasp

154 2mm 18 karat gold faceted beads

 21 8mm by 3mm faceted disc-shaped London
     blue topaz beads

NOTE:

Using the thinner .013 wire instead of .015
allows you to use a micro-crimp bead. Because
this bead is almost invisible beside the little
faceted beads, you can avoid using crimp covers.
If you use .015 wire and regular crimps, you
should add crimp covers.

PINK SAPPHIRE AND GOLD-FILLED NECKLACE

(PICTURED ON PAGE 74-75)

REDDISH TONES SEEM TO ENHANCE THE LOOK OF GOLD, INCREAS-
ING ITS IMPACT. THE PINK SAPPHIRES IN THIS SIMPLE DESIGN
ADD RICH GLOW TO THE MODEST AND INEXPENSIVE GOLD-FILLED
ROUND BEADS.

1. Start the necklace by threading on a micro-crimp. Pass the
   beading wire through the ring of one half of the clasp and back
   through the crimp. Add one 2mm by 2mm crimp and pass it over
   the micro-crimp. Make sure that the beading wire is tight around
   the ring and squeeze the crimps shut using the crimping pliers.

2. Thread on seven gold-filled beads and a pink sapphire bead. Add
   three gold-filled beads and a sapphire. Repeat this pattern
   twenty-five times or until the necklace is the length you wish.
   (Remember to try it around your neck to make sure.)

3. Add a final set of seven gold beads, a micro-crimp, and a 2mm by
   2mm crimp. Bring the beading wire through the ring of the other
   side of the clasp and back through the crimp and round bead.
   Now tighten the necklace so there are no spaces between the
   beads. Close the crimp and snip off any remaining beading wire.
   Finish off by adding the crimp covers.

TOOLS

Wire Cutters, Crimping Pliers

MATERIALS

2   gold-filled micro-crimp beads

20" of .013 beading wire (Note: I have
    used .013 wire instead of .015 because
    of the very small hole size of the pink
    sapphires)

1   9mm round, gold filled box clasp

2   2mm by 2mm gold-filled crimps

92 2.5mm gold-filled seamless round
    beads

27 9mm by 9mm pink sapphire box-cut
    briolette

2   gold-filled crimp covers

SILVER CHAIN AND WIRE NECKLACE

THE SIMPLE ELEGANCE OF SILVER AND BLACK IS TRANSFORMED HERE INTO AN EXTRAVAGANT DISPLAY. EACH TYPE OF CHAIN IS AN INTEGRAL PART OF THE DESIGN RATHER THAN JUST A STRAND LINKING THE WIRE-WRAPPED BEADS. THE RUTILATED QUARTZ AND SQUARE SWAROVSKI CRYSTAL BEADS ADD THEIR OWN DISTINCTIVE CHARACTER TO THE BASIC BLACK AND SILVER THEME.

1. Cut the wire into twelve pieces that are 2" long and fourteen pieces that are 2¹/₂" long. Use them to create wire-wrapped, double-ended pendants of all the beads (except the Swarovski squares) as follows:

2. (A) 2" wire, 3mm silver round, 5mm daisy, 14mm onyx, 5mm daisy, 3mm silver round

3. (B) 2¹/₂" wire, 2mm silver round, 4mm daisy, 8mm onyx, 4mm daisy, 2mm silver round

4. (C) 2¹/₂" wire, 2mm silver round, 19 7mm silver bead, 2mm silver round

TOOLS
Wire Cutters, Round-Nosed Pliers, Flat-Nosed Pliers

MATERIALS

59"	of 22-gauge silver wire
8	3mm seamless hollow silver round beads
8	5mm silver daisy spacer beads
4	14mm faceted black onyx round beads
44	2mm seamless hollow silver round beads
22	4mm silver daisy spacer beads
5	19mm by 7mm silver antiqued rectangular beads
12	8mm faceted black onyx round beads.
5	faceted rutilated quartz oval beads 8mm wide and between 10mm and 16mm long
5	14mm by 14mm Swarovski crystal square (style 4439) beads
11	9mm silver 19-gauge jump rings
10	5mm silver twisted wire rings
13"	of silver cable chain with 5mm links (SC)
1	silver with marcasite toggle clasp
50	4mm silver 19-gauge jump rings
15"	of silver cable chain with flattened 7mm links (LC)

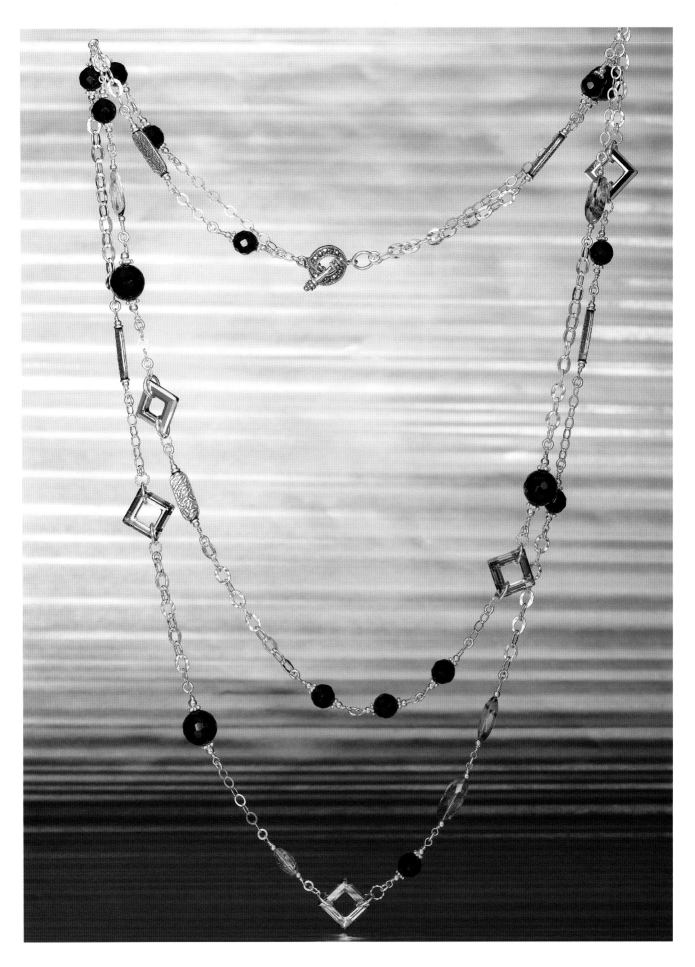

SILVER "TUSK" NECKLACE

SHELL BEADS FROM THE NAGA TRIBES OF NORTHERN INDIA AND BURMA, ALONG WITH AN ORGANIC-LOOKING GEMSTONE SUCH AS JASPER, MATCHES THE TEXTURED, ALMOST ORGANIC FEEL OF THE SILVER "TUSK." JASPER COMES IN MANY VARIETIES OF PATTERN AND COLOR, SOME UNIQUE TO SPECIFIC MINES. THIS PARTICULAR ONE IS CALLED FIRE JASPER BECAUSE OF ITS GLOWING RED COLORATION. IF YOU CANNOT FIND THIS VARIETY, YOU COULD SUBSTITUTE OTHER JASPERS AND RETAIN THE SAME FEELING.

1. Thread the silk onto the beading needle. Double it and tie a double knot at the end. Put a dab of hypo-cement or nail polish on the knot and cut the tail very close to the knot. Thread on one half of the clasp so that the knot sits inside the ring. Tie another knot tightly against the outside of the clasp and then begin adding the beads.

2. Thread on two jasper beads (J), a larger (6mm) silver bead (LS), four J, one small (4mm) silver bead (SS), a turquoise nugget, SS, make a knot, J, LS, Naga shell bead, silver "tusk," 3mm red coral bead, Naga shell, SS, three J. Make a knot, LS, seven J, LS, J, SS, 6mm turquoise disc, SS, four J, LS, J. Make a knot.

3. Thread on the other half of the clasp. Make a knot and use your awl to get it tightly against the inside of the ring of the clasp. Make another knot on top of it and tighten it firmly. Add a dab of hypo-cement or clear nail polish and cut away the remaining thread.

TOOLS

Beading Needle, Awl, Hypo-Cement or Clear Nail Polish

MATERIALS

36"	of size F silk
1	silver hook-and-eye clasp
22	8mm "fire" jasper round beads (J)
5	6mm Thai silver disc beads (LS)
5	4mm Thai silver disc beads (SS)
1	35mm by 18mm (approximately) Chinese turquoise nugget bead
2	17mm Naga shell with inlaid turquoise round beads
1	100mm (approximately) Thai silver tusk-shaped bead
1	3mm red coral bead
1	6mm Chinese turquoise disc bead

NOTE

Hill tribe design styles are highly respected although often idiosyncratic. Here, I have used the spirit of hill tribe design to showcase an impressive Thai silver "tusk." Although you need a degree of courage to use large pieces like this in jewelry, the result can be very rewarding.

SWEET SIXTEEN NECKLACE

(PICTURED ON OPPOSING PAGE, LEFT)

14-INCH CHOKER, PERFECT FOR THAT FIRST REAL STRAND OF PEARLS

Follow the instructions for knotting on silk (page 16) and using basket bead tips (page 20). Attach one part of the clasp. Knot on enough beads to make about 13 inches of length, and try the strand around your neck. Remember to allow for the length of the clasp. Knot on a few more pearls as necessary to get the right length. Try it again. Attach the bead tip, keeping everything nice and snug. Put on the other half of the clasp. Voila!

TOOLS

Beading Needle, Awl, Scissors

MATERIALS

65 4.5mm round light cream-colored pearls (about four-fifths of a 16" strand)

 2 gold-filled basket bead tips

 1 gold-filled box clasp, 10mm long

 2 yds of size F silk

THE CLASSIC NECKLACE

(PICTURED ON OPPOSING PAGE RIGHT)

WHAT EVERY WOMAN NEEDS

Follow the instructions for stringing on silk (page 16) and using French wire (page 24). Attach one part of the clasp. Knot on enough beads to make about 15 inches of length, and try the strand around your neck. Knot on a few more pearls as necessary to get the right length, keeping in mind that your last three beads will only be knotted after attaching the French wire. Attach the other half of the clasp using the rest of the French wire.

TOOLS

Beading Needle, Awl, Scissors

MATERIALS

54 7mm round white freshwater pearls (a little less than a 16" strand)

2 ¼" pieces of silver French wire

 1 sterling silver box clasp (shown here with a mabe pearl)

 2 yds of size F silk

BIG-GIRL PEARLS NECKLACE

(PICTURED OPPOSING PAGE, CENTER)

WHAT EVERY WOMAN WANTS

Follow the instructions for stringing on silk (page 16) and using clamshell bead tips (page 18). Attach one part of the clasp. Knot on enough beads to make about 15 inches of length, and try the strand around your neck. Remember to allow for the length of the clasp. Knot on a few more pearls as necessary to get the right length. Try it again, and then add the other half of the clasp.

TOOLS

Beading Needle, Awl, Flat-Nosed Pliers, Scissors

MATERIALS

42 9mm round cream Akoya pearls (a little less than a 16" strand)

 2 gold-filled clamshell bead tips

 1 gold hook-and-eye clasp 20mm long

 2 yds of size F silk

THE CLASSIC THREE-STRAND NECKLACE

THIS STYLE WAS A FAMOUS FAVORITE OF JACQUELINE KENNEDY ONASSIS. TO MAKE IT, YOU MUST BE CAREFUL TO GET EACH OF THE THREE STRANDS THE CORRECT LENGTH. THE SECOND AND THIRD STRANDS MUST HAVE MORE PEARLS THAN THE FIRST SO THAT THE THREE LIE PARALLEL TO ONE ANOTHER AND DON'T OVERLAP WHEN ATTACHED TO THE CLASP.

1. Make the first knotted strand, using enough beads to make about 14 inches of length (see "Getting Knotted," page 16). This particular clasp adds more than an inch to the overall length of the necklace. If you choose another clasp that adds less, you can increase the length of the pearl strand. Using the bead tip, attach one end of the strand to the top row of one side of the clasp. Try it around your neck to see if it is long enough. If it is the right length, finish it off with a basket bead tip and attach it to the top row of the other half of the clasp.

2. Make the second knotted strand a bit longer than the first, with two more pearls than you used on the first strand. Attach one end of the strand to the middle row of the clasp. Try the necklace on. If you hold the knot of the last pearl to the ring of the clasp, the two rows should just touch. If the second strand overlaps the first, add another bead (or more) until the strands form two parallel lines. When the length is right, use a bead tip to finish off, and attach the end to the middle row of the other part of the clasp.

3. Make the third knotted strand a bit longer than the second, with one more pearl than you used on the second one. Attach one end of the strand to the third row of the clasp. Try the necklace on, holding the knot of the last pearl to the ring of the clasp. The rows should just touch. If they overlap, add another pearl (or more) until the rows form three parallel lines. When the length is right, use a bead tip to finish off the strand, and attach it to the third row of the other part of the clasp.

TOOLS
Beading Needle, Awl, Scissors

MATERIALS

3   16" strands of semi-baroque 8mm Akoya pearls. (You will have some pearls left over, possibly enough for a bracelet and definitely plenty for matching earrings.)

1   sterling silver 3-row clasp set with marcasite (a metallic gemstone)

8   yds of size F white silk thread

6   sterling silver basket-bead tips

NOTE
Test the length of each strand around your neck before you attach it to the clasp to be sure it doesn't overlap the others or create a large gap between them. Since the pearl sizes will vary a bit, this measuring method is the only way to be sure to get the three strands the proper length.

MULTISTRAND KESHI PEARL NECKLACE

THIS NECKLACE IS DESIGNED SO THAT THE STRANDS OF PEARLS OVERLAP AND CLUSTER TOGETHER. IT COMBINES SMALL KESHI PEARLS, WHICH CAN BE FAIRLY INEXPENSIVE, WITH TINY GOLD-PLATED CHARLOTTE SEED BEADS FOR A STUNNING EFFECT. THE PATTERN IS QUITE RANDOM; USE YOUR OWN JUDGMENT ABOUT HOW TO MIX BEADS, OR SEE THE PHOTO ON PAGE 87.

1. To get seven strands onto a five-row clasp, the two outside rows are doubled. To make one of these doubled strands, start with 42 inches of beading wire. Fold it in half. Pass the folded V-shape end of the wire through a crimp and attach to the top loop of one side of the clasp. Now string on your charlottes and pearls until the strand is 16 inches long. Put tape around the end of the beading wire to keep the beads from falling off. Fill the other side of the doubled wire with charlottes and pearls. Make the strand 16 1/4 inches long. Holding the two wire ends so that the beads can't fall off, remove the tape and insert both ends into a crimp bead. Bring the wire through the top loop of the other half of the clasp and back through the crimp. Before you squeeze the crimp shut, adjust the wires so the beads are snug with no gaps between them. The first wire will be a bit shorter than the second, so tighten them accordingly.

2. To make the third strand, cut 20 inches of beading wire. Attach one end to the second row of the clasp and fill it with pearls and charlottes to a length of 16 1/2 inches. Make sure the beads are snug, and attach it to the next row of the clasp. Repeat this for the fourth strand, increasing the length of pearls and charlottes to 16 3/4 inches, and attaching the fourth strand to the middle row of the clasp. Repeat for the fifth strand, attaching it to the fourth row of the clasp to make a length of 17 inches.

3. Make the sixth and seventh strands using the doubled-wire technique. The first line of this doubled strand should have 17 1/4 inches of pearls and charlottes, and the second 17 1/4 inches. The longer length goes at the bottom of your necklace.

TOOLS

Wire Cutters, Crimping Pliers

MATERIALS

- 5 16" strands of small side-drilled keshi pearls in the 3–4mm size range
- 3 20" strands (or 5 grams) of gold-plated charlotte beads, size 13/0. Charlottes are little glass beads that have an irregular cut on one side and are then gold plated
- 10 gold-filled crimp beads
- 10 gold-filled crimp bead covers
- 13 ft of .015 49-strand beading wire

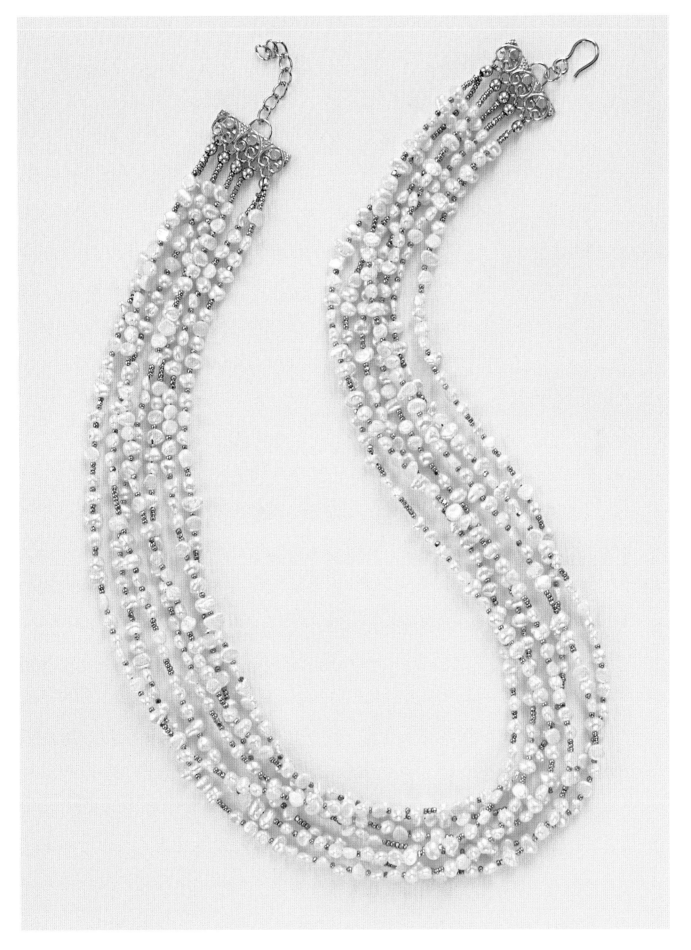

DOUBLE-STRAND NECKLACE

FEEL FREE TO VARY THE RANDOM PATTERN OF PEARLS AND CRYSTALS IN THIS NECKLACE TO SUIT YOUR OWN SENSE OF SYMMETRY. DOUBLE AB-COATED CRYSTALS HAVE AN IRIDESCENT FINISH ("AB" STANDS FOR AURORA BOREALIS) THAT GIVES THE NECKLACE REFLECTIONS. IF YOU USE DIFFERENT COLORS OF PEARLS, USE CRYSTAL BEADS THAT MATCH THEM.

1. Cut the beading wire into two equal lengths. Start the first strand by threading on a crimp bead. Pass the beading wire through the loop of the clasp and back through the crimp. Tighten the wire around the loop and close the crimp. Add the two gold beads and the crystal bead to cover the tail of the wire. Snip off any of the tail that protrudes from the crystal bead. Then, string a series of beads as follows: 1 gold bead, 2 green pearls, 1 crystal, 5 pearls, 1 crystal, 13 pearls, 1 crystal, 3 pearls, 1 crystal, 8 pearls, 1 crystal, 9 pearls, 1 crystal, 8 pearls, 1 crystal, 6 pearls, 1 crystal, 1 pearl, 1 crystal, 10 pearls, 1 crystal, 8 pearls, 1 crystal, 5 pearls, 1 crystal, 11 pearls, 1 crystal. The pearls should fit snugly together, each facing opposite its neighbor. Check the length around your neck, remembering that the strand will get shorter when you twist it. Add enough pearls to achieve the necessary length (the distance from pearl to pearl should be about 16 inches). Then add 1 gold bead, 1 crystal, 2 gold beads, and a crimp. Finish the strand by attaching it to the loop of the other side of the clasp.

2. Make the second strand the same way as the first, but at each end, use a pattern of 1 gold bead, 1 crystal, then 2 gold beads. Try to arrange the crystal beads so they do not lie exactly opposite those on the first strand. The number of pearls, starting from the same side as the first strand, is as follows: 2, 4, 5, 3, 5, 6, 6, 7, 1, 6, 5, 3, 6, 5, 5, 2, 5, 3. Adjust the final number of pearls so that the second strand is approximately the same length as the first. Attach the finished second strand to the clasp. Attach the crimp covers to all the crimps. To wear, twist the necklace a few times until you achieve a look that pleases you.

TOOLS

Wire Cutters, Crimping Pliers

MATERIALS

1	16" strand of 5 by 6mm dyed green top-drilled teardrop pearls
1	16" strand of 6 by 8mm dyed light blue top-drilled teardrop pearls
34	4mm double AB-coated light sapphire Swarovski bicone crystal beads
12	gold-filled 3.5mm round beads
4	gold-filled crimp beads
4	gold-filled crimp bead covers
40"	beading wire
1	large (17mm) vermeil toggle clasp

NOTE:
When a double strand is twisted, it becomes shorter. Although the overall length of this design is almost 18 inches, when twisted, it is a standard short length.

If the teardrop pearls are arranged tightly on the strands, they will fall naturally to opposite sides.

CRYSTAL AND PEARL NECKLACE

THE TINY SILVER-PLATED CHARLOTTES IN THIS THREE-STRAND NECKLACE ARE JUST A LITTLE OVER A MILLIMETER IN SIZE, BUT THEY SERVE AN IMPORTANT PURPOSE: THEY FRAME EACH OF THE SWAROVSKI CRYSTAL BEADS, EMPHASIZING THEIR BICONE SHAPE AND GIVING THEM SPACE TO CREATE AN IMPRESSION.

1. Cut the beading wire into two pieces, one measuring 20 inches and the other 44 inches. Divide the crystals into three groups of 26, 28, and 30 beads, respectively. Use the crimp to attach the shorter length of beading wire to the clasp loop. String 3 silver charlotte spacers, then alternate pearls with the set of 26 crystals to fill the rest of the strand to about 15 1/2 inches. Remember to put a silver spacer bead on either side of each crystal! If you're not confident about creating a random pattern right on the wire, arrange the beads in a row first until you are happy with the grouping. Try the strand around your neck to test its size. Check to make sure each crystal has one spacer bead on each side. If you finish the necklace and then find you missed even one sequence of spacer, crystal, spacer, it will ruin your day! Finish by adding 3 more spacer beads and a crimp and attaching the strand to the other side of the clasp.

2. Take the long strand of beading wire and fold it in half. Pass the folded "V"-shape end of the wire through a crimp and attach to the top loop of one side of the clasp. Using the instructions above, string a strand of pearls and crystals with the group of 28 crystals. Make this strand 1 inch longer than the first strand. As you add your beads, lay them alongside the first strand to make sure that the random patterns are harmonious. Check for length (and to make sure that all the crystals have spacers on either side), and attach the strand to the other half of the clasp.

3. Make the final strand 1 inch longer than the second strand, using the remaining pearls, spacers, and the final 30 crystals. Check the size and the spacers; attach the strand to the clasp.

TOOLS
Wire Cutters, Crimping Pliers

MATERIALS

2	16" strands of 2–3mm rondel white freshwater pearls
84	4mm tanzanite Swarovski crystal bicone beads
196	silver-plated charlottes (14/0)
6	sterling silver crimp beads
1	10mm sterling silver toggle clasp
64"	beading wire

NOTE
The three strands of this necklace, although different lengths, are attached to the loops of a single row clasp so that they stand out as three separate rows when worn.

FACETED PEARLS ON WIRE NECKLACE

WHEN YOU USE EITHER GOLD-FILLED OR STERLING SILVER WIRE, IT BECOMES AN INTEGRAL PART OF THE DESIGN. IN THIS DESIGN, THE LUSTER OF THE FACETED PEARLS HAS GEM-LIKE REFLECTIONS. (ALL FACETED PEARLS ARE FRESHWATER SINCE THEY NEED TO HAVE VERY THICK NACRE.) THE COLORS OF THE LITTLE DANGLES OF GEMSTONE BRIOLETTES ARE ARRANGED ASYMMETRICALLY, WHICH GIVES THE NECKLACE A DYNAMIC LOOK. FEEL FREE TO SELECT COLORS THAT SUIT YOUR TASTE.

1. Start by making the pearl links. Use 1 ½ inches of gold-filled wire for each pearl and create a 3- to 3.5-millimeter loop on either side (see "Wire-Wrapping," page 23.) Cut only a couple of pieces of wire at the beginning to test the optimum length for your pearls.

2. When you have finished the links, use the headpins to make the tiny dangles. Put on 1 gemstone briolette and 1 gold bead, then make a 2- to 2.5-millimeter loop and wrap the remaining wire around the base of the loop.

3. Start making the necklace by taking 1 of the wrapped pearls and adding an open jump ring to one end. Slip another wrapped pearl onto the jump ring and close it. Repeat this process 2 more times.

4. After adding the open jump ring to the fourth pearl, slip on 1 of the gemstone dangles. Add the next pearl and close the jump ring (see illustration). Repeat this pattern 17 times. Now add 4 more pearls and jump rings without any dangles. Add a final open jump ring. Slip on the last of your gemstone dangles, then the spring ring clasp, and close the jump ring. When you wear your necklace, the clasp will attach to the loop at the end of the first wire-wrapped pearl.

TOOLS
Wire Cutters, Round-Nosed Pliers, Flat-Nosed Pliers

MATERIALS
- 25 5.5mm faceted freshwater pearls (about a third of a 16" multicolor strand)
- 19 4–5mm multicolor tourmaline briolettes
- 25 3.5mm gold-filled jump rings
- 19 ½" gold-filled headpins
- 19 2.5mm gold-filled round beads
- 1 6mm gold-filled spring ring clasp
- 40" gold-filled 24-gauge wire

A LOT OF WORK—
BUT WORTH IT! NECKLACE

THIS NECKLACE REALLY DOES TAKE A LONG TIME TO MAKE, BUT IT ALSO ATTRACTS A LOT OF ENTHUSIASTIC ADMIRATION WHEN WORN. ALTHOUGH NEITHER THE PEARLS NOR THE LITTLE GEMSTONES ARE COSTLY, THE ALL-NATURAL COLORS AND ELABORATE CONSTRUCTION OF THIS DESIGN MAKE IT LOOK LIKE A VERY EXPENSIVE PIECE OF JEWELRY.

1. Start by making the little pendants, using the same method for each. Take a headpin and add a mixture of baroque pearls, gemstones, and gold beads and spacers. (Use the photograph on page 79 as inspiration for appealing mixtures.) Then make a wire-wrapped loop about 2 to 3 millimeters in diameter. The secret to this design is that the length of the pendants varies from ³/₈ to ⁷/₈ of an inch. This prevents them from clashing when they are on the necklace. I suggest you make equal numbers of the pendants in 3 lengths—long, medium, and short. Or you can line the dangles up as you make them to see how they will fit together.

2. Using the crimp backed by a 3-millimeter gold bead, attach the beading wire to the clasp. Add 1 daisy spacer, 1 round pearl, and 1 pendant. Repeat the round-pearl-and-pendant pattern until you have used up all your pendants. Hold the necklace up frequently to make sure that the arrangement of the pendants is working well. Check the length of the necklace around your neck. Finish off with 1 pearl, 1 spacer, and 1 round gold bead, and attach the end to the other half of the clasp with a crimp. Add the crimp covers. Go out to dinner to show off the result of all your work!

TOOLS
Wire Cutters, Crimping Pliers , Round-Nosed Pliers, Flat-Nosed Pliers

MATERIALS

1	16" strand of 5.5mm near-round natural pink-color freshwater pearls
1	16" strand of 5–7mm mixed natural and dyed color baroque pearls
1	mixture of "leftover" small gemstones and pearls (garnet, rainbow moonstone, iolite)
40	4mm vermeil daisy spacer beads
12	assorted other 4mm vermeil spacers and bead caps
12	2mm gold-filled round beads
67	1" gold-filled head pins
2	gold-filled crimp beads
2	3mm gold-filled round beads
2	gold-filled crimp bead covers
1	15mm vermeil toggle clasp
20"	beading wire

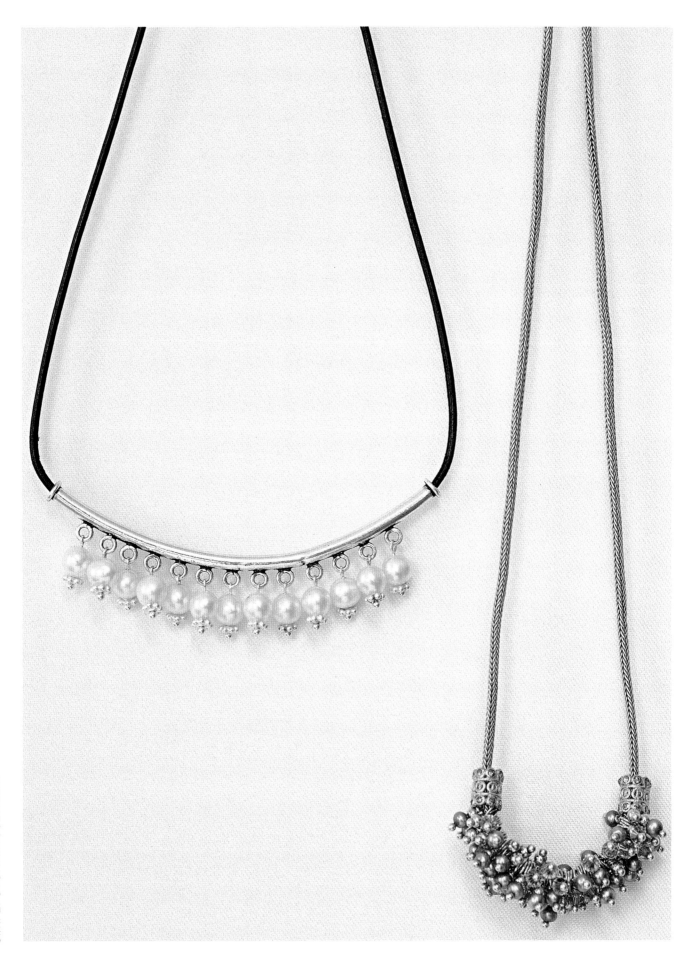

PEARLS ON LEATHER CORD NECKLACE

CORDS ARE TOO THICK TO THREAD THROUGH PEARLS, BUT THEY CAN BE USED EFFECTIVELY TO DISPLAY THEM.

1. First make the 13 pearl drops (see "Using Headpins and Eyepins," page 22). Add 1 silver daisy to a headpin, followed by 1 pearl. Make a small loop. Repeat until you have 13 drops. When you have finished all the drops, hook them onto the silver cord tube by opening and closing the loops.

2. Attach half the clasp to the end of the leather cord by squeezing the crimp part with flat-nosed pliers. Slide on the silver tube. Try it around your neck for size and finish off by attaching the other half of the clasp.

TOOLS

Round-Nosed Pliers, Flat-Nosed Pliers

MATERIALS

- 13 6mm white near-round freshwater pearls
- 13 4mm sterling silver daisy spacer beads
- 13 2$^1/_2$" sterling silver headpins with ball tips
- 1 sterling silver cord tube with 13 loops
- 1 sterling silver leather crimp clasp
- 16" 1.5mm leather cord (European quality)

PEARLS ON SNAKE CHAIN NECKLACE

THE GOLD CORD ALSO KNOWN AS SNAKE CHAIN COMES WITH THE CLASP ALREADY ATTACHED. ONE SIDE OF THE CLASP UNSCREWS TO LET YOU STRING THE BEADS ONTO THE CORD.

1. First make all the little dangles by attaching a bead or beads to a headpin and making a small loop (see page 22). Use your own judgment to create a variety of different types of dangles: a single pearl; a single crystal; a single gold bead; 1 pearl and 1 gold bead; 1 crystal bead and 1 gold bead. (See the photo on page 96 for guidance.) The loops should have a short wrap. As you make them, be sure that the loops are big enough to slide on to the gold cord.

2. Unscrew the clasp. Add 1 gold tube bead, and then arrange all the dangles in a pleasing manner. Add the other gold tube bead, and screw the clasp back on.

TOOLS

Round-Nosed Pliers

MATERIALS

- 42 3mm freshwater pearls with natural purple hue
- 32 3mm light amethyst Swarovski crystal bicone beads
- 32 gold-filled 2.5mm round beads
- 77 gold headpins with ball tip
- 2 7 by 5mm gold tube beads
- 1 16" gold snake chain with unscrewing hook-and-eye clasp attached

KESHI PEARL NECKLACE

THESE TWO NECKLACES HAVE THE SAME DESIGN BUT USE
PEARLS AND SPACER BEADS IN DIFFERENT SHAPES. VARYING
THE INGREDIENTS IN ANY OF THESE DESIGNS GIVES YOU A
PIECE OF JEWELRY THAT IS UNIQUELY YOURS.

1. Attach the beading wire to the ring using the crimp bead (see
    "Using Crimp Beads to Attach Clasps," page 14). Add the crimp
    cover. Add 1 large gold bead and 1 pearl. The sequence of beads
    is random, so you feel free to create your own version. If you
    want to replicate the exact design from the photo on page 98,
    follow this pattern (see abbreviations in ingredients list):

    *   d, 3r, d, p, d, r
    *   d, p, d, r, large gold bead
    *   r, d, p, d, r, f, r, f, r, large gold bead
    *   r, f, p, f, r, f, p, d, 8r, large gold bead, p, r
    *   f, p (repeated a total of 4 times), f, r
    *   f, p (repeated a total of 3 times), large gold bead, p, f, r
    *   f, p (repeated a total of 6 times)
    *   f, d, 3r, f, r, f, r, d, p, f,
    *   p, 3f, p, f, r, f, p, f, p, d, r, d, p
    *   Large gold bead, p, d, r, large gold bead, r, d, p, large gold
        bead, and a crimp bead

2. To make the loop, add the following pattern after the crimp: 7 r,
    d, r, f, 8r, f, r, f, r, f, 2r, f. Pass the wire back through the crimp and
    the large gold bead. Close the crimp and snip off the remaining
    wire as close to the gold bead as possible.

3. Make 10 little dangles with the assorted gemstones and small
    round gold beads. Make 6 of them by adding 1 gemstone and 1
    gold bead to a headpin. Make 2 more using a combination of 1
    gemstone, 1 gold bead, 1 gemstone, and 1 gold bead. Make the
    final 2 dangles with a arrangement of 1 gemstone and 3 gold
    beads. Hook all the dangles onto the bottom of the gold ring,
    where you started the lariat, by opening and closing the loops.

TOOLS
Crimping Pliers, Wire Cutters,
Round-Nosed Pliers

TO MAKE A 21-INCH LARIAT

29 large keshi pearls about 14mm in
    size, about a 16" strand (abbreviated as
    "p" in recipe)

51 4mm hand-cut faceted ruby rondels, about
    half a 16" strand (abbreviated as "r" in
    recipe)

8 9mm gold-filled hollow round beads

15 4mm gold-filled daisy spacer beads
    (abbreviated as "d" in recipe)

34 2mm gold-filled faceted beads (abbreviated as "f" in recipe)

1 5mm gold-filled soldered ring

10 assorted 4mm gemstone beads in red
    tones for the end tassel

6 2mm and six 3mm gold-filled round beads
    for the end tassel

10 $2^1/_2$" gold-filled headpins with ball tip for
    the end tassel

2 gold-filled crimp beads

2 gold crimp covers

26 inches of beading wire

PRESSED GLASS AND CRYSTAL NECKLACE

ALTHOUGH PRESSED GLASS BEADS ARE MORE ECONOMICAL THAN LAMPWORK BEADS, THEY CAN NONETHELESS BE USED TO CREATE EQUALLY ELEGANT AND SOPHISTICATED JEWELRY. THIS NECKLACE RELIES ON TWO COMPLEMENTARY TONES FOR ITS EFFECT—ONE, A SIMPLE BUT PLEASANT BLUE; THE OTHER, A LIGHT GREEN WITH A MOTTLED AMBER COATING KNOWN AS A PICASSO FINISH. THE LITTLE "DAGGER" SHAPES REQUIRE SPACER BEADS BETWEEN EACH TO ENSURE THEY HANG PROPERLY. USING A TINY AMBER CRYSTAL BEAD ADDS A DASH OF SPARKLE AT THE BASE OF THE MAIN GLASS BEADS WHILE SERVING AS A SPACER. USING SILVER BEADING WIRE ADDS REFLECTIVITY TO THE TRANSPARENT CRYSTAL BEADS FOR EXTRA SHINE AND INTEREST.

1. Start the necklace by threading on a crimp. Pass the beading wire through the ring of one half of the clasp and then back through the crimp. Make sure that the beading wire is tight around the ring. Squeeze the crimp shut with crimping pliers.

2. Thread on three 2mm silver beads.

3. Now add a crystal bead, a blue pressed glass bead, another crystal bead, and then a mottled green pressed glass bead. Repeat this pattern fifty-two times; then, add the final blue pressed glass bead.

4. Check the necklace around your neck to make sure that it is the right length. Add three 2mm silver beads and one crimp. Bring the beading wire through the ring of the other side of the clasp and then back through the crimp and round bead. Now, tighten the necklace so there are no spaces between the beads, close the crimp, and snip off any remaining beading wire. Add the crimp covers.

TOOLS
Wire Cutters, Crimping Pliers

MATERIALS

107	3mm x 10mm pressed glass top-drilled dagger shaped beads in two colors—
53	mottled green and 54 blue
108	2mm round Swarovski crystal beads
6	2mm silver hollow seamless round beads
1	sterling silver hook and eye clasp
2	silver crimp beads
2	silver crimp bead covers
20"	of silver beading wire

SILVER CHAIN AND LAMPWORK NECKLACE

THESE BEAUTIFUL GLASS BEADS ARE DESIGNED AND MADE BY CZECH ARTIST ALENA CHLADKOVA. TRANSPARENT BANDS OF GLASS ARE LAID AS RIDGES ON THE CENTRAL CORE, GIVING TEXTURE AND INTERESTING LIGHT EFFECTS TO THE BEADS. THIS NECKLACE IS A CLASSIC EXAMPLE OF HOW FINE DESIGN AND THE INDIVIDUAL MERIT OF EACH HAND-CRAFTED BEAD CALL FOR A SETTING OF SOLID SILVER.

1. Start by attaching each of the glass beads to a piece of looped wire in the following manner: Using your round-nosed pliers, make a simple loop at one end of the silver wire. Thread a silver bead onto the wire; then, add a glass bead and another silver bead. Make sure they are snug against one another and against the loop; then, cut the wire about ¼" above the last bead. Make a simple loop, ensuring that the bottom of the loop fits snugly against the round bead. Repeat this process for the rest of the silver and glass beads.

2. Cut the chain into twenty-two pieces, each three links long. (Tip: For each piece, you will have one unused link. Save all these cut links, along with any other scraps of silver wire your work generates. When you have collected enough of this "waste," you can take it to a smelter and collect on the value of the silver.)

3. Arrange your glass beads in a pleasing manner. The pattern I have used is as follows: barrel, 12mm round, rectangle, 10mm round, 12mm round, B, 10mm, R, B, 12mm, 10mm, R, B, 12mm, R, 10mm, B, 12mm, B, R, 12mm, 10mm. Attach a glass bead to the end of a piece of chain by opening the loop, slipping it on the end link of the piece of chain, and then closing it. Attach the next glass bead to the other end of the chain. Continue adding beads and chain lengths until you have used them all. To complete the loop, attach the end link of the chain to the other side of the glass bead you started with.

TOOLS
Wire Cutters, Round-Nosed Pliers, Flat-Nosed Pliers

MATERIALS (TO MAKE A 28" ROPE LENGTH)

5   10mm round lampwork glass beads

6   12mm round lampwork glass beads

5   14mm x 16mm flat rectangular lampwork glass beads (R)

6   16mm x 9mm barrel lampwork glass beads (B)

44 2.5mm seamless hollow silver beads

12" silver chain with 5mm oval links

30" 20 gauge silver wire

TIP: Working the wire this way is far less wasteful than cutting preset lengths of wire. Because the beads are different sizes, they will use different lengths of wire. If you cut each piece from the whole length of wire as you make it, you will have almost no waste at the end.

GRADUATED DICHROIC GLASS CHOKER

ONE USUALLY THINKS OF ROUND BEADS WHEN DESIGNING
GRADUATED NECKLACES, BUT IRREGULAR SHAPES CAN ALSO
WORK WELL. ONE THEORY BEHIND THE APPEAL OF GRADUATED
NECKLACES, ESPECIALLY IN THE CASE OF PEARLS AND OTHER
GEMS, IS THAT THE SMALLER, CHEAPER BEADS ARE BEHIND THE
NECK, OFTEN UNDER YOUR HAIR, AND THUS NOT AS VISIBLE.
GRADUATED NECKLACES ARE NOT JUST FOR ECONOMY, HOWEVER;
THEY HAVE A VISUAL APPEAL OF THEIR OWN, INCREASING THE
SENSE OF PERSPECTIVE AND DRAWING THE EYE ALONG THE
NECK.

1. Start by arranging your dichroic beads on a bead board or soft
   fabric surface. Put the largest bead in the center and the next
   two largest beads on either side. Continue adding pairs of
   slightly smaller beads on either side of the central ones until you
   have used all the beads. Now, check the arrangement to make
   sure the color pattern is pleasing and the graduated effect is
   apparent.

2. Thread a crimp onto the beading wire. Pass the wire through the
   ring of one half of the clasp and then back through the crimp.
   Make sure that the beading wire is tight around the ring.
   Squeeze the crimp shut. Add two 3mm gold round beads to cover
   the tail of the beading wire and cut away any visible excess wire.

3. Thread on a 4mm gold bead and the first of your dichroic beads.
   Continue in this manner until you have used all the dichroic
   beads. Try the necklace to check the pattern and length.

4. Add a 4mm gold bead, two 3mm beads, and a crimp. Bring the
   beading wire through the ring of the other side of the clasp and
   then back through the crimp and one or two of the round beads.
   Now, tighten the necklace so there are no spaces between the
   beads, close the crimp, and snip off any remaining beading wire.
   Add the crimp covers.

TOOLS
Wire Cutters, Crimping Pliers

MATERIALS

21	13mm dichroic glass beads from 9mm to 18mm in size
22	4mm gold-filled hollow seamless faceted round beads
4	3mm gold-filled hollow seamless round beads
2	gold-filled crimp beads
2	gold-filled crimp covers
1	vermeil toggle clasp
22"	of beading wire

SEED BEAD THREE-STRAND NECKLACE

SINCE SEED BEADS ARE VERY SMALL, IT IS COMMON TO INCORPORATE MULTIPLE STRANDS INTO A PIECE TO CREATE A BIGGER IMPRESSION. THE ELEGANT SILVER CONE AT THE END OF THIS NECKLACE GIVES THE SEED BEADS A MORE SOPHISTICATED LOOK. THE BEADS SPILL OUT FROM THE SILVER LIKE A SMALL CORNUCOPIA.

1. Cut the silver wire into two 3" pieces. Make a wire-wrapped loop (page 23) at one end of each piece. Wrap several times around the base of each loop—the loops need to be strong enough to hold the three strands of beads.

2. Thread a crimp onto the beading wire. Pass it through one of the loops you just made and then back through the crimp. Tighten the beading wire on the loop and squeeze the crimp shut, cutting away any excess beading wire. Now thread on fifteen seed beads.

3. Add a rondel and seven seed beads. Repeat this pattern thirty-seven times; then, add another fifteen seed beads and a crimp. Pass the wire through the loop of the other piece of silver wire and then back through the crimp. Make sure all of the beads are tight against one another. Close the crimp. Cut away the balance of the wire.

4. Make the second strand exactly the same way as the first, but start and finish with only thirteen seed beads.

5. Make the third strand exactly the same way as the first, but start and finish with only eleven seed beads.

6. Pass the unlooped end of one of the pieces of silver wire through the wide end of a cone and out through the hole at the narrow end. Add a 3mm silver bead to the wire, and make a simple loop (page 23). Open the loop and attach it to one half of the clasp. Repeat the procedure to attach the other end of the necklace to the clasp.

TOOLS
Wire Cutters, Crimping Pliers

MATERIALS (FOR A 21" NECKLACE)
(about) 900 size 11/0 seed beads

117	4mm faceted glass rondels
2	44mm x 6mm silver curved cones
2	3mm silver hollow seamless round beads
1	10mm silver toggle clasp
6	silver crimp beads
6"	of 20 gauge silver wire
66"	of beading wire

SWAROVSKI CRYSTAL NECKLACE

SWAROVSKI HAS BEEN A DRIVING FORCE IN GLASS JEWELRY FOR MANY YEARS. WITH FINISHED JEWELRY AND COMPONENTS DIVISIONS, AS WELL AS RETAIL STORES, SWAROVSKI HAS A STRONG UNDERSTANDING OF FASHION AND GOES TO GREAT LENGTHS TO BOTH FOLLOW AND INFLUENCE IT.

EVERY YEAR, SWAROVSKI PRODUCES NEW COMPONENT DESIGNS, ONE OF WHICH IS THE RECENTLY INTRODUCED CRYSTAL RING, OR DONUT SHAPE. WITH ALL THE OUTSIDE EDGES, THE DONUT PROVIDES A GLITTERING ACCOMPANIMENT TO OTHER CRYSTAL BEADS AND WORKS PARTICULARLY WELL AS THE LINKING COMPONENT OF A LARIAT NECKLACE. BOTH TYPES OF CRYSTAL ARE IN THE CRYSTAL COPPER COLOR, BUT A DOZEN OTHER COLORS COULD BE USED TO SIMILAR EFFECT.

1. Cut a 4" piece from the beading wire. Thread a crimp onto this piece and add thirteen round crystal beads. Pass the wire through a 14mm donut and then back through the crimp. Arrange the beads so they make a nice tight loop around the edge of the donut. Push enough beading wire through the crimp so you can add another thirteen round beads. Pass this part of the wire through another 14mm donut and then back through the crimp again. Arrange the beads so they make a nice tight loop around the edge of the donut. Make sure both loops are well shaped and the beads are snug. With the beginning of the wire just through the crimp, squeeze the crimp firmly shut. Cut away the balance of the wire.

2. Repeat this process to add another 14mm donut to the last one.

3. Thread a crimp onto the remaining beading wire. Add seventeen round crystal beads. Pass the wire through the 20mm donut and then back through the crimp. Arrange the beads so they make a nice tight loop around the edge of the donut. When you are sure that all the beads are fitting snugly together, place the tail of the wire just through the crimp and squeeze the crimp shut.

4. Add about 23" of round crystal beads—but make sure you have thirteen beads left for the final loop. When you are happy with the length, add a crimp and the thirteen round crystal beads. Pass the wire through the end donut of the 14mm donut group and then back through the crimp. Arrange the beads so they make a nice tight loop around the edge of the donut. When all the beads in the necklace are snug against one another, squeeze the crimp shut. Add the crimp covers. To wear this lariat, simply double the strand back through the large ring.

TOOLS
Wire Cutters, Crimping Pliers

MATERIALS
- 1 20mm Swarovski donut
- 3 14mm Swarovski donuts
- 540 2mm round Swarovski crystal beads (style 5000)
- 4 gold-filled crimp beads
- 4 gold-filled bead covers
- 35" of beading wire

CRYSTAL AND SILVER CHAIN NECKLACE

BLUES AND GREENS TEND TO GO WELL WITH SILVER: THESE ARE THE PREDOMINANT COLORS IN THIS NECKLACE. I HAVE USED A SMALLER NUMBER OF AMBER TONES TO ADD A LITTLE WARMTH TO THE DESIGN. EACH ONE OF THE OCTAGONAL CRYSTAL BEADS IS LARGE AND IMPRESSIVE AND BALANCES WELL AGAINST THE LARGE LINKS OF THE HEAVY SILVER CHAIN. THE SHAPE OF THE LINKS IS SIMILAR TO THAT OF THE BEADS AND CREATES A HARMONIOUS APPEARANCE—A SIMPLE DESIGN TO BE SURE, BUT ONE THAT IS ELEGANT AND DISTINGUISHED.

1. Start by attaching each of the crystal beads to a piece of looped wire in the following way: Use your round-nosed pliers to make a simple loop at one end of the silver wire. Thread a silver torus bead onto the wire and then add a crystal bead and another silver bead. Make sure the beads are snug against one another and against the loop; then, cut the wire about ¼" above the last bead. Make a simple loop, ensuring that the bottom of the loop fits tightly against the round bead. Repeat this process for the rest of the silver and crystal beads.

2. Cut the chain into thirteen pieces; each piece should be three links long.

3. Attach a crystal bead to the end of a piece of chain by opening the loop, slipping it on the end link of the piece of chain, and then closing it. Attach the next crystal bead to the other end of the chain. Continue adding beads and chain until you have used them all.

4. Add the last piece of chain to the end crystal bead. Use the jump rings to attach half of the clasp to each end of the necklace.

TOOLS
Wire Cutters, Round-Nosed, and Flat-Nosed Pliers

MATERIALS

12	18mm x 10mm Swarovski crystal beads
24	4mm silver torus spacer beads
28"	of silver chain with heavy 11mm x 7mm links (or enough for 13 sections of 3 links each when cut)
15"	20 gauge silver wire
1	22mm x 13mm oval toggle clasp

VENETIAN GLASS NECKLACE

VENICE IS THE GREAT HISTORICAL CENTER OF GLASS BEAD-MAKING. ALTHOUGH THE AMOUNT OF GLASS PRODUCED THERE IS NOW RELATIVELY SMALL, VENICE'S PRODUCTS AND DESIGN INNOVATIONS ARE AS GREAT AS EVER, CONSEQUENTLY DRIVING UP THE PRICE OF GENUINE VENETIAN GLASS. SADLY, FEW VISITORS TO VENICE EVER SEE REAL VENETIAN GLASS BEADS, AS TOURIST SHOPS AND EVEN SPECIALTY BEAD STORES HAVE TAKEN TO SELLING FAR CHEAPER COPIES FROM THE CZECH REPUBLIC, CHINA, AND INDIA. WHILE THE FOREIGN COPIES ARE SOMETIMES VERY, VERY GOOD, NOTHING COMPARES TO THAT INEFFABLE QUALITY THAT SEEMS TO BE THE VERY HEART OF THE VENETIAN STYLE.

THE BEADS IN THIS NECKLACE SEEM SO SIMPLE—GOLD FOIL WRAPPED IN FROSTED, TRANSLUCENT ITALIAN GLASS. YET BOTH THEIR TEXTURE AND THEIR COLOR ARE PERFECTLY DELIGHTFUL, AND NO ONE WILL EVER MISTAKE THEM FOR ANYTHING LESS THAN THE VALUABLE VENETIAN GLASS BEADS THEY ARE. IT IS SAID THAT TRULY AUTHENTIC ITALIAN CUISINE DOES NOT TRAVEL ONE METER OUTSIDE THE BORDER OF ITALY; VENICE'S TALENT FOR PRODUCING UNIQUELY DELICIOUS BEADS LIKEWISE REMAINS REMOTE.

1. Make a simple loop at one end of the gold-filled wire. Add a bead cap (convex side facing the loop); then, add a glass bead and another bead cap (concave side facing the bead). Cut the wire about ¼" above the bead cap, and make a simple loop. Repeat this procedure with the rest of the glass beads and bead caps.

2. Use the 5mm split rings to join all of the wired glass beads together in a chain; then, add a 7mm split ring to each end. Attach the hook clasp to one of the 7mm split rings.

TOOLS

Wire Cutters, Crimping Pliers, Round-Nosed Pliers, Flat-Nosed Pliers

MATERIALS

24	12mm round Venetian lampwork glass beads with interior gold foil
48	4mm gold-filled beads caps
24	5mm gold-filled split rings
2	7mm gold-filled split rings
1	16mm vermeil hook clasp
24"	of 20 gauge gold-filled wire

LAMPWORK GLASS WITH PEWTER NECKLACE

BECAUSE THESE LOVELY LAMPWORK GLASS BEADS BY NANCY PILGRIM ARE "FUMED," OR SMOKED WITH MICROSCOPIC GOLD FILM, THEY CALL FOR A GOLD ACCOMPANIMENT. BUT WHAT DO YOU DO IF YOUR BUDGET DOES NOT ALLOW FOR GOLD-FILLED OR VERMEIL BEADS? THE ANSWER IS GOLD-PLATED PEWTER, AN ALLOY COMPOSED MAINLY OF TIN. THE INTERESTING SHAPE OF THE LITTLE PEWTER CHARMS DRAMATICALLY CHANGES THE LOOK OF THE NECKLACE AND ENHANCES THE APPEARANCE OF THE GLASS RONDELS.

1. Thread a crimp onto the beading wire. Pass the beading wire through the ring of one half of the clasp and then back through the crimp. Make sure that the beading wire is tight around the ring. Squeeze the crimp shut. Thread on a 2.5mm bead, a 3mm bead, a 6mm glass bead, a 3mm bead, a 2.5mm bead, and another 3mm bead.

2. Add a 12mm rondel, a 3mm bead, a 2.5mm bead, a pewter charm, a 2.5mm, and a 3mm bead. Repeat the pattern twenty-four times.

3. Try the necklace on for size. Add a 3mm bead, a 2.5mm bead, a 3mm bead, a 6mm glass bead, a 3mm bead, a 2.5mm bead, and a crimp. Bring the beading wire through the ring of the other side of the clasp and then back through the crimp and the round bead. Now, tighten the necklace so there are no spaces between the beads, close the crimp, and snip off any remaining beading wire. Add the crimp covers.

TOOLS
Wire Cutters, Crimping Pliers

MATERIALS

25	12mm rondel "fumed" lampworkglass beads
2	6mm lampwork glass beads
24	6mm x 10mm gold-plated pewter charms.
54	3mm gold-filled hollow seamless round beads
52	2.5mm gold-filled hollow seamless round beads
1	14mm gold-plated toggle clasp
2	gold-filled crimp beads
2	gold-filled bead covers
20"	of gold colored beading wire

ENAMEL CENTERPIECE NECKLACE

ENAMEL IS A GLASS-LIKE FILM FUSED TO A METAL, CERAMIC, OR GLASS BASE. TRADITIONAL, OR VITREOUS, ENAMEL IS PRODUCED WHEN POWDERED GLASS, OFTEN IN THE FORM OF A PASTE, IS HEATED TO A HIGH TEMPERATURE ON THE BASE MATERIAL TO PRODUCE A THIN LAYER OF SOLID GLASS. THIS TRADITIONAL ENAMEL CENTERPIECE IS BY SUSAN KNOPP.

1. Thread on a crimp. Pass the beading wire through the ring of half of the clasp and back through the crimp. Make sure that the beading wire is tight around the ring. Squeeze the crimp shut.

2. Thread two 2.5mm beads, a 5mm Thai silver bead, and a dichroic bead. Now add a 2.5mm bead, a 5mm bead, a 2.5mm bead, a 10mm rondel, a 2.5mm bead, a 5mm bead, a 2.5mm bead, and a 12mm glass bead. Repeat this pattern (A) once more; then, add a 2.5mm bead, a 5mm bead, a 2.5mm bead, and a 12mm glass bead. Repeat this pattern (B) once more; then, add a 2.5mm bead, a 5mm bead, a 2.5mm bead, a dichroic bead, a 2.5mm bead, a 5mm bead, a 2.5mm bead, a 10mm rondel, a 2.5mm bead, a 5mm bead, a 2.5mm bead, and a dichroic bead. Repeat pattern B. Then, repeat pattern A twice. Add a 2.5mm bead, a 5mm bead, a 2.5mm bead, a dichroic bead, a 2.5mm bead, and a 5mm bead to complete the first side of the necklace.

3. Add the ten Thai silver chips and pass the wire through the top of the centerpiece. Complete the other side of the necklace as a mirror image of the first. Pass the beading wire through the ring of the other half of the toggle clasp and then back through the crimp. Now, tighten the necklace so there are no spaces between the beads, close the crimp, and snip off any remaining beading wire. Add the crimp covers.

4. To make the little dangle, add a dichroic bead, a 2.5mm bead, and a crystal bead to the 1" headpin. Make a wire-wrapped loop to attach to the bottom of the centerpiece. Add a crystal to each of the two ¹/₂" headpins and make simple loops to attach them to the loop of the larger dangle.

TOOLS
Wire cutters, Crimping Pliers

MATERIALS

1	46mm enamel on silver centerpiece
14	12mm round lampwork with inside silver foil beads
10	10mm rondel lampwork with inside silver foil beads
9	8mm round dichroic beads
34	5mm Thai silver beads
10	3 to 4mm Thai silver chips
70	2.5mm silver hollow seamless round beads
3	2mm round crystal beads
2	¹/₂" silver headpins with ball tip
2	1" silver headpin with ball tip
1	24mm hook and eye clasp
1	silver crimp bead
1	silver crimp bead cover
22"	of beading wire

GLASS THAT GLITTERS LIKE GOLD NECKLACE

SOME GLASS BEADS ARE SO SENSATIONAL THAT SOLID GOLD IS THEIR NATURAL PARTNER. THESE BEAUTIFUL BEADS ARE MADE BY AMERICAN GLASS BEAD ARTIST SCOTT TURNBULL. HIS SPECIALTY IS USING THE IRIDESCENT QUALITIES OF DICHROIC GLASS. HERE HE HAS COMBINED IT WITH 23-KARAT GOLD LEAF TO CREATE AN EFFECT RICH ENOUGH TO BE COMPLEMENTED BY THE GOLD OF THE HOLLOW CUBE BEADS.

1. Start the necklace by threading on a crimp. Pass the beading wire through the ring of one half of the clasp and then back through the crimp. Make sure that the beading wire is tight around the ring. Squeeze the crimp shut. Add a 2.5mm gold round bead to cover the tail of the beading wire and cut.

2. Now thread on a gold cube bead, a 1.5mm round bead, a dichroic glass bead, and another 1.5mm round bead. Repeat this pattern twenty-two times or until the necklace is the length you wish. (Remember to try the necklace on to make sure you've reached the right length.)

3. Add a final gold cube bead, a 2.5mm round bead, and a crimp. Bring the beading wire through the ring of the other side of the clasp and then back through the crimp and round bead. Now, tighten the necklace so there are no spaces between the beads, close the crimp, and snip off any remaining beading wire. Add the crimp covers to the crimps.

TOOLS
Wire Cutters, Crimping Pliers

MATERIALS

23	13mm dichroic glass round beads with interior gold
24	5mm 18 karat gold hollow cube beads.
2	2.5mm 18 karat gold-filled hollow seamless round beads
46	2mm 18 karat gold-filled hollow seamless round beads
2	gold-filled crimp beads
2	gold-filled crimp covers
1	18-karat gold toggle clasp
20"	of beading wire

NOTE
Sometimes the holes of lampwork glass beads are so large that they do not sit snugly on the beading wire but move around in an unattractive way. The solution is to use tiny round beads that fit into the holes of the lampwork beads. I have used that solution in this necklace. The 2mm beads are hardly seen, as they are covered by the holes of the glass beads, but they are essential to making the necklace work properly. If you were using glass beads with smaller holes, they would not be necessary. If the holes are so large that the little gold beads do not hold them properly, put some seed beads on the wire between the gold beads so the dichroic beads fit over them and are kept from moving around.

THREE-IN-ONE PRESSED GLASS AND SILVER NECKLACE

EACH OF THE THREE STRANDS OF THIS NECKLACE IS FINISHED AT BOTH ENDS WITH A SPRING RING CLASP SO THEY CAN BE WORN AS INDIVIDUAL NECKLACES OR USED AN EYEGLASS LEASH.

1. For strand 1: Use the silver wire to wire wrap the following combinations: 3x (H, E, H); 3x (H, F, BF, H); 2x (H, A, A, A, H); 1x (H, D, G, B, G, D, H); 2x (H, C, H); 1x (H, A, A, A, A, A, A, H); 2x (H, G, D, D, D, G, H); 1x (H, B, H); 1x (H, G, D, G, H). Cut the silver chain into ten 1" pieces and seven ½" pieces. Use the jump rings to join the pieces of chain to the wire-wrapped pieces so that every wire-wrapped piece is separated by chain. Attach the spring ring clasps to the ends of the chain using two more jump rings. Make six dangles with the headpins and remaining rondels (D), and then attach them at random to several jump rings.

2. For strand 2: Thread a crimp onto the beading wire; pass the wire through the loop of the clasp and then back through the crimp. Squeeze the crimp shut. Thread on a 2.5mm silver bead (H). Now add 28 charlotte beads (J), a bead cap (F), an 8mm (B), and another bead cap (F). Repeat this pattern 16 more times and then add a final group of 28 charlotte beads. Add a 3mm silver bead and a crimp; attach to the other side of the clasp.

3. For strand 3: Thread a crimp onto the beading wire; pass the wire through the loop of the clasp and then back through the crimp; squeeze the crimp shut. Thread on the following: S, 7J, B, 7J, S, 3A, S, 7J, S, K, S, 3J, S, B, S, 3J, S, K, S, 7J, S, 5A, S, 3J, B, 3J, S, D, S, 5J, H, E, H, 5J, S, J, S, K, S, J, S, K, S, J, S, K, S, J, S, C, S, 5J, S, J, B, J, S, 5J, S, D, S, D, S, D, S, 7J, S, 3A, S, 7J, S, J, S, K, S, J, S, B, S, J, S, K, S, J, S, 7J, S, 5A, S, 5J, H, E, H, 5J, S, J, B, J, S, 5J, S, 3A, S, 5J, S, K, S, J, S, 5J, S, C, S, J, S, K, S, J, S, 7J, S, B, S, J, S, B, S, J, S, B, S, 7J, S, D, S, 3J, S, H, E, H, 9A. Now, using the last set of leaf-shaped beads as the center point, reverse the pattern to copy it so the other side of the necklace matches the first. Add a crimp, and attach the strand to the final spring ring clasp. Hook all of the spring ring clasps onto the 8mm silver ring to create the three. To connect all: an 8mm silver spring ring.

TOOLS
Wire Cutters, Crimping Pliers

MATERIALS
Strand 1
- 11   10mm pressed glass leaf-shaped beads (A)
- 6   8mm round pressed glass beads (B)
- 3   7mm x 8mm fire-polished faceted pressed glass bead (F)
- 13   4mm x 6mm facetted rondel pressed glass beads (D)
- 3   6mm silver decorated rondel beads (D)
- 6   7mm silver decorated bead caps (F)
- 12   4mm silver daisy spacer beds (G)
- 39   2.5mm silver hollow round beads (H)
- 6½"   headpins with ball tips
- 34   4mm silver jump rings
- 2   6mm silver spring ring clasps
- 30"   of 26 gauge silver wire
- 16"   of silver chain with 3mm links

Strand 2
- 17   8mm round pressed glass beads (B)
- 2   12" strands of size 13/0 charlotte seed beads (J)
- 34   7mm silver decorated bead caps (F)
- 2   2.5mm silver hollow round beads (H)
- 2   6mm silver spring ring clasps
- 2   silver crimp beads
- 2   silver bead covers
- 34"   of beading wire

Strand 3
- 47   10mm pressed glass leaf-shaped beads (A)
- 18   8mm round pressed glass beads (B)
- 18   4mm flat faceted disc pressed glass beads (K)
- 13   4mm x 6mm facetted rondel pressed glass beads (D)
- 4   7mm x 8mm fire-polished faceted pressed glass bead (C)
- 6   6mm silver decorated rondel beads (E)
- 1   12" strand of size 13/0 charlotte seed beads (J)
- 125   size 13/0 silver plated charlotte seed beads (S)
- 12   2.5mm silver hollow round beads (H)
- 2   6mm silver spring ring clasps
- 2   silver crimp beads
- 2   silver bead covers
- 36"   of beading wire

GLASS AND GOLD CHAIN ADJUSTABLE NECKLACE

THIS IS A WONDERFUL WAY TO USE THE MANY EXTRA GLASS BEADS YOU WILL ACCRUE OVER TIME. IF YOU DON'T HAVE A VARIETY OF LEFTOVER BEADS, THEN AN ENTERTAINING HOUR IN A GOOD OPEN-DISPLAY BEAD STORE WILL GIVE YOU THE SELECTION YOU NEED TO MAKE THIS NECKLACE.

MANY TYPES OF GLASS BEADS ARE REPRESENTED HERE—LAMPWORK, PRESSED GLASS, DICHROIC, CRYSTAL, EVEN VINTAGE BEADS. WHEN YOU SELECT YOUR BEADS, YOU NEED ONLY TO MAKE SURE THAT THE COLOR TONES ARE SIMILAR. THE REDS AND PINKS OF THIS NECKLACE ARE PERFECTLY SUITED TO GOLD CHAIN. IF YOU PREFER TO USE SILVER CHAIN, TRY CHANGING THE COLOR TONES TO BLUES AND GREENS.

1. First, make all the dangles. For each one, select a glass bead. If the hole is a little large, use one of the 2mm or 3mm round beads, a daisy spacer, or a bead cap on the headpin. Add a spacer, a round gold bead, or both above the bead. On three of the dangles, I have used glass bead caps on top of the central bead. I have made one of the dangles with the vermeil charm by cutting the ball from the headpin, making a simple loop to hold the ring of the charm, adding a small glass bead, and finishing with another simple loop.

2. Using the jump rings, make the cluster at the end of the chain. Add one of the larger, more impressive beads to the end link of the chain; then, add two smaller dangles to the next link and two more to the link after that. If you have a double-ended component like the one in this design, cut the chain about 4" from the start and use two jump rings to join it back together with the double-ended component in between.

3. Leave another 3" of the chain empty; then, add a dangle to every other link. If you have some very small dangles, you can add them to the same links as those which already have a larger dangle—but only in a few places. Leave about 3" of chain empty after the last dangle. Add the hook clasp. To wear, simply put the hook through one of the empty links at the beginning of the necklace to create your desired length.

TOOLS
Round-Nosed Pliers, Flat-Nosed Pliers

MATERIALS
- 42 assorted glass beads of a red/pink or neutral color tone, from 4mm to 18mm
- 3 assorted glass bead caps from 10mm to 14mm
- 1 11mm vermeil disc charm
- 2 7mm silver daisy spacer beads
- 20 4mm vermeil daisy spacer beads
- 10 assorted gold-filled spacer beads
- 4 5mm vermeil bead caps
- 44 4mm gold-filled jump rings
- 30 3mm gold-filled hollow seamless round beads
- 30 2mm gold-filled round beads
- 1 11mm x 15mm vermeil hook clasp
- 42 1" gold-filled headpins with ball tips
- 28" of gold-filled cable chain with 6mm x 8mm links

TRIANGULAR TOURMALINE NECKLACE

TOURMALINE IS TRIGONAL, WHICH MEANS THAT ITS LONG CRYSTALS HAVE A TRIANGULAR CROSS SECTION. TO MAKE THESE LOVELY AND UNUSUAL BEADS, THE CUTTER HAS TAKEN ADVANTAGE OF THE NATURAL SHAPE AND ADDED LONG FACETS THE LENGTH OF THE CRYSTAL THAT PROVIDE AN INTRIGUING REFLECTIVE PATTERN. BECAUSE OF ITS MANY COLORS, TOURMALINE CAN TAKE ON VARIOUS PERSONALITIES. THIS GREEN-BLUE COMBINATION IS QUIETLY ELEGANT, DISPLAYING THE OBVIOUS RICHNESS OF JEWELS IN A DISCREETLY UNDERSTATED FASHION.

IF THE TEMPORARY STRAND OF TOURMALINE IS ARRANGED IN A PLEASING MANNER, YOU CAN PLACE THE TOURMALINE BEADS IN THE ORDER THEY COME OFF THAT STRAND. IF NOT, THEN LAY OUT THE BEADS IN A LINE AND ARRANGE THEM HOW YOU WISH. PUT THE MOST IMPRESSIVE BEADS TOWARD THE CENTER AND THE LESS STRIKING ONES AT THE ENDS, WHERE THEY ARE HIDDEN BEHIND THE NECK.

1. Start the necklace by threading on a crimp. Pass the beading wire through the ring of one half of the clasp and back through the crimp. Make sure that the beading wire is tight around the ring and squeeze the crimp shut.

2. Thread on a 2mm gold bead so that it fits over the tail of the wire. Cut away the excess tail.

3. Add a pearl, a daisy spacer bead, a tourmaline bead, and another daisy spacer. Repeat this pattern 39 times or until the necklace has reached the length you desire.

4. Add a final pearl, the 2mm gold bead, and a crimp. Bring the beading wire through the ring of the other side of the clasp and back through the crimp and the gold bead. Tighten the necklace so that there are no spaces between the beads. Close the crimp and snip off any remaining beading wire. Add the crimp covers.

TOOLS
Wire Cutters, Crimping Pliers

MATERIALS

1   12" strand of triangular tourmaline beads approximately 7mm in diameter (the beads vary in length). Note: These strands often come in 14" lengths, allowing some beads to be left over for earrings.

41   2.5mm pearls (or one more than the number of tourmaline beads)

80   3mm 18 karat gold daisy spacer beads (or twice the number of tourmaline beads)

2   2mm hollow gold-filled round beads

1   18 karat gold hook-and-eye clasp

2   gold-filled crimp beads

2   gold-filled crimp bead covers

20"   of beading wire (gold color is preferable)

TURQUOISE AND HESSONITE NECKLACE

THESE TUMBLED DROPS OF CHINESE TURQUOISE HAVE A BEAUTIFUL COLOR AND FORM AN EXTRAVAGANT FRAME FOR THE DRAMATIC PATTERNS OF THE CENTRAL PENDANT.

ALTHOUGH SOME TURQUOISE IS PURE BLUE, MOST IS INTERSPERSED WITH BROWN OR BLACK VEINS OF OTHER MINERALS, A FEATURE THAT OFTEN GIVES IT A MORE INTERESTING CHARACTER. HESSONITE, A TYPE OF GARNET, HAS A RICH MAPLE SYRUP HUE WHICH PICKS UP AND EMPHASIZES THE HONEY BROWN VEINS OF THE TURQUOISE.

1. First make the pendant loop. Decide which is the back of the pendant bead. Pass the beading wire through the front of the pendant, then add a hessonite bead and a crimp so that they are at the back of the pendant. Add a hessonite and a daisy. Repeat 5 times and add the final hessonite. Pass the wire back through the front of the pendant, the hessonite bead, the crimp, and the next hessonite bead. Now tighten the loop so that all the beads are snug. There must be about 3mm to 4mm of space between the top of the pendant bead and the top of the loop.

2. Thread a crimp on the beading wire. Pass the wire through the ring of one half of the clasp and back through the crimp. Make sure that the beading wire is tight around the ring and squeeze the crimp shut. Thread on three 3mm silver beads so that they fit over the tail of the wire and cut off any excess.

3. Thread on a hessonite bead, a silver daisy, a turquoise bead, and another daisy.

4. Add a hessonite, daisy, turquoise, daisy, turquoise, daisy, turquoise, daisy, hessonite, daisy, turquoise, daisy, turquoise, daisy, turquoise, daisy, turquoise daisy, turquoise, and daisy. Repeat this pattern 2 more times. Then add a hessonite, daisy, turquoise, daisy, turquoise, daisy, turquoise, daisy, hessonite, 3 daisies, and a 3mm silver round bead.

5. Add the pendant loop, then reverse the directions in steps 3 and 4 to make the other half of the necklace a mirror image of the first. Add 3 round silver beads and the crimp. Bring the beading wire through the ring of the other side of the clasp and back through the crimp and silver round bead. Tighten the necklace so that there are no spaces between the beads, close the crimp, and snip off any remaining beading wire. Add the crimp covers.

TOOLS
Wire Cutters, Crimping Pliers

MATERIALS

56	top-drilled Chinese turquoise tumbled drops approximately 15mm to 20mm in length
1	25mm by 48mm Chinese turquoise pendant bead
25	3mm hessonite round beads
83	4mm silver daisy spacer beads
8	3mm seamless hollow silver round beads
1	silver toggle clasp
3	silver crimp beads
2	silver crimp bead covers
24"	of beading wire

NOTE
Depending on where the hole is drilled in your pendant bead, you may need more or fewer hessonite and daisy beads to make the pendant loop.

TURQUOISE AND HESSONITE NECKLACE

TOPAZ AND "CORNFLAKES" NECKLACE

THIS NECKLACE IS A FINE EXAMPLE OF HOW MODERN
ENHANCEMENTS HAVE INCREASED THE PALETTE OF THE
JEWELRY DESIGNER. "LONDON BLUE" TOPAZ DID NOT EXIST
UNTIL MODERN IRRADIATION TECHNIQUES WERE DEVELOPED.

1. First, arrange your topaz beads so that the largest bead is at the
    center and the smallest are at either end. The two beads on
    either side of the central bead should be of equal size and the
    whole arrangement should be balanced so that all opposing
    topaz beads match each other as closely as possible.

2. Start the necklace by threading on a crimp. Pass the beading
    wire through the ring of one half of the clasp and back through
    the crimp. Make sure that the beading wire is tight around the
    ring and squeeze the crimp shut.

3. Thread on 2 round gold beads so that they fit over the tail of the
    wire and cut away any excess. Then add 9 charlotte beads.

4. Using the arranged topaz beads, add a round gold bead, a Thai
    vermeil chip, a topaz bead, a vermeil chip, a gold round, 3
    charlottes, a pearl, a charlotte, a pearl, a charlotte, another pearl,
    and 3 charlottes. Repeat this pattern 4 more times.

5. Now add 2 more charlottes, a round gold, a vermeil chip, and a
    topaz bead. Add another vermeil chip and then the central topaz
    bead. Add another vermeil chip, a topaz bead, a vermeil chip,
    a round gold, and 2 charlottes.

6. Now reverse the order in step 4 to make the other half of the
    necklace a mirror image of the first.

7. Add 9 charlottes, a gold round, and a crimp. Bring the beading
    wire through the ring of the other side of the clasp and back
    through the crimp and the round bead. Tighten the necklace so
    that there are no spaces between the beads, close the crimp, and
    snip off any remaining wire. Add the crimp covers.

TOOLS
Wire Cutters, Crimping Pliers

MATERIALS

13	oval-shaped "London Blue" topaz beads ranging in size from 8mm by 7mm to 11mm by 10mm
30	silver peacock, top-drilled cornflake pearls approximately 13mm in diameter
24	Thai vermeil chips approximately 4mm in diameter
84	size 13 gold-plated charlotte beads
22	2mm hollow gold-filled round beads
1	vermeil toggle clasp
2	gold-filled crimp beads
2	gold-filled crimp bead covers
20"	of beading wire

SMOOTH AQUAMARINE NECKLACE

AQUAMARINE USED TO BE PRIZED FOR ITS "SEA-GREEN" COLOR, BUT AS TASTES HAVE TURNED TO TROPICAL BLUE WATER, SO HAS THAT COLOR BECOME MORE POPULAR. THE LOVELY PINK FORM OF THE STONE IS ALSO PROPERLY CALLED "MORGANITE" (NAMED AFTER THE AMERICAN BANKER AND COLLECTOR OF GEMSTONE, J.P. MORGAN), BUT IT SOUNDS A LOT MORE ROMANTIC TO CALL IT "PINK AQUAMARINE." ALL OF THEM ARE PRECIOUS BERYL. MOST AQUAMARINE IS HEAT-TREATED TO TRY TO ACHIEVE THE CURRENT IDEAL PALE BLUE COLOR, BUT THESE LOVELY STONES ARE NATURAL. THE CLOUDY NATURE COULD BE SEEN AS A LACK OF CLARITY, BUT FOR ME, IT GIVES THE STONE A DELIGHT-FUL CHARACTER THAT I FIND MORE INTERESTING THAN THE CLEAR VARIETY. THE CLOUDINESS HAS THE OTHER BENEFIT OF MAKING SUCH LARGE STONES MORE AFFORDABLE BECAUSE IF CLEAR AQUAMARINE GEMS WERE THIS HUGE, THEY WOULD BE HUGELY EXPENSIVE.

1. Unless the strand you have bought is strung exactly the way you want it, start by laying out the stones in a color and size arrangement that pleases you. Start the necklace by threading on a crimp. Pass the beading wire through the ring of one half of the clasp and back through the crimp. Make sure that the beading wire is tight around the ring and squeeze the crimp shut.

2. Thread on a gold round bead so that it fits over the tail of the wire and cut away any excess. Then add 4 more gold beads. Add the gemstone beads in the order in which they are laid out, putting 3 gold beads between each gemstone. Try the necklace around your neck to make sure that the length and color arrangement please you.

3. Add another 5 gold beads and a crimp. Bring the beading wire through the ring of the other side of the clasp and back through the crimp and the round bead. Now tighten the necklace so that there are no spaces between the beads, close the crimp and snip off any remaining beading wire. Add the crimp covers.

TOOLS
Wire Cutters, Crimping Pliers

MATERIALS (FOR A 22" NECKLACE)

1   18" strand of graduated aquamarine in smooth, tumbled shapes ranging from 13mm to 33mm in size

70   2mm 18 karat gold round beads

1   18 karat box clasp

2   gold-filled crimp beads

2   gold-filled crimp bead covers

26"   of beading wire

DIAMONDS IN THE ROUGH NECKLACE

UNTIL A FEW YEARS AGO, DIAMONDS WERE THE EXCLUSIVE PROVINCE OF PROFESSIONAL JEWELERS WHO NEEDED TO SET THEM IN PRECIOUS METAL BEFORE THEY COULD BE USED. DIAMONDS ARE 140 TIMES HARDER THAN THE NEXT HARDEST GEMSTONE AND DRILLING THEM WAS NOT AN OPTION. THE INVENTION OF THE LASER DRILL, HOWEVER, HAS AT LAST MADE POSSIBLE THE CREATION OF DIAMOND BEADS. UNFORTUNATELY, TECHNOLOGY HAS NOT MADE THESE DESIRABLE GEMS ANY LESS EXPENSIVE AND THE VISION OF A ROPE OF CUT AND POLISHED DIAMONDS IS STILL ONLY A REALITY FOR THE VERY RICH AND A DREAM FOR THE REST OF US. BUT SMALL, ROUGH DIAMONDS CAN BE BOUGHT FOR HUNDREDS OF DOLLARS A STRAND RATHER THAN HUNDREDS OF THOUSANDS. ALTHOUGH THEY EXPRESS ONLY THE OCCASIONAL FLASH OF DIAMOND SPARKLE, ROUGH DIAMONDS HAVE A DISTINCTIVE CHARACTER, SUBTLE BUT STILL EMPHATIC. LIKE ALL DIAMONDS, THESE HAVE INVESTMENT VALUE, SO YOU HAVE THE PLEASURE OF WEARING YOUR WEALTH AROUND YOUR NECK.

1. Start the necklace by threading on a crimp. Pass the beading wire through the ring of one half of the clasp and back through the crimp. Make sure that the beading wire is tight around the ring and squeeze the crimp shut.

2. Add a gold bead and then a few diamond beads. The gold beads are going to be scattered among the diamond beads in a random fashion. So you don't use up the gold beads too quickly, divide them into 3 equal portions and use 1 portion for each of the diamond strands. For an idea of random spacing, refer to the picture of the necklace. Save 1 gold bead as the last bead before the crimp. Add all the diamond beads, separating them at random points with 1 or 2 gold beads.

3. Add the final gold bead and a crimp. Bring the beading wire through the ring of the other side of the clasp and back through the crimp. Tighten the necklace so that there are no spaces between the beads, close the crimp, and snip off any remaining beading wire.

TOOLS
Crimping Pliers, Wire Cutters

MATERIALS (FOR A 49" ROPE)
- 3   14" strands of 3mm rough diamond beads
- 1   7" strand of 2mm 18 karat gold faceted round beads
- 1   18 karat gold hook-and-eye clasp
- 1   4mm 18 karat gold ring
- 54" of size 0.13 beading wire

GREEN KYANITE SHARDS NECKLACE

THE NAME *KYANITE* COMES FROM THE GREEK WORD FOR "BLUE," BUT AS YOU CAN SEE IN THIS NECKLACE, THE STONE IS SOMETIMES FOUND IN PLEASANT SHADES OF GREEN. I HAVE USED A GRADUATED STRAND OF SHARDS THAT, ROUGHLY CUT AND POLISHED, GIVES AN IMPRESSION OF THE NATURAL CRYSTAL. THIS KYANITE IS NEITHER HIGH QUALITY NOR VERY EXPENSIVE, BUT THE UNUSUAL COLOR AND SHAPE OF THE SHARDS, AS WELL AS THEIR BROAD SURFACE AREA, HELP MAKE THIS A PARTICULARLY INTERESTING GEMSTONE DISPLAY.

1. Start the necklace by threading on a crimp. Pass the beading wire through the ring of one half of the clasp and back through the crimp. Make sure that the beading wire is tight around the ring and squeeze the crimp shut.

2. Thread on a silver round bead so that it fits over the tail of the wire and cut away any excess. Add a black onyx bead and a faceted silver bead. Repeat this 3 times and add an additional black onyx bead.

3. Take the first kyanite bead off the temporary strand and add it to the wire followed by a black onyx bead. Repeat this with the rest of the kyanite beads, being sure to thread them on so that the graduation remains the same as it was on the temporary strand and that there is a black onyx bead after each kyanite shard.

4. Add a faceted silver bead and a black onyx bead. Repeat 3 times and then add the remaining silver round bead and a crimp. Bring the beading wire through the ring of the other side of the clasp and back through the crimp and the round bead. Tighten the necklace so that there are no spaces between the beads, close the crimp, and snip off any remaining beading wire. Add the crimp covers.

TOOLS
Wire Cutters, Crimping Pliers

MATERIALS
1   14" graduated strand of green kyanite with shards from 10mm to 35mm long

60   2mm black onyx round beads (You might need a few more or less depending on the number of kyanite shards.)

2   2.5mm hollow silver round beads

8   2mm faceted silver spacer beads

1   silver toggle clasp

2   silver crimp beads

2   silver crimp bead covers

20"   of beading wire

WHEN BLACK IS BRILLIANT NECKLACE

THERE ARE SEVERAL BLACK GEMSTONES, INCLUDING HEMATITE, BLACK ONYX, OBSIDIAN, AND JET, THE LAST GIVING ITS NAME TO THAT ULTIMATE DARKNESS, "JET BLACK." ALTHOUGH THEIR ABSENCE OF COLOR IS SIMILAR, THEY ARE DIFFERENTIATED BY THEIR LUSTER, AND IT IS BLACK SPINEL THAT, WITH THE EXCEPTION OF BLACK DIAMOND, OWNS THE TOP POSITION IN THE SPARKLE CATEGORY. SPINEL IS A HARD STONE WITH VERY GOOD REFLECTIVITY; THE RED VARIETY WAS PREVIOUSLY THOUGHT TO BE A TYPE OF RUBY AND EQUALLY PRIZED. IN THE BLACK VERSION OF THE STONE, QUALITY DEPENDS ON EXCELLENT CUTTING TO MAXIMIZE ITS WONDERFUL REFLECTIVE PROPERTIES.

TOOLS
Wire Cutters, Crimping Pliers

MATERIALS

26 10mm by 10mm flattened heart-shaped black spinel briolettes

189 (about a 14" strand) 1mm by 1mm faceted Thai silver beads

1 silver "stardust" toggle clasp

2 silver crimp beads

2 silver crimp bead covers

20" of beading wire

1. Start the necklace by threading on a crimp. Pass the beading wire through the ring of one half of the clasp and back through the crimp. Make sure that the beading wire is tight around the ring and squeeze the crimp shut. Cut off any tail of the wire as close to the crimp bead as possible.

2. Thread on 7 silver beads and a spinel briolette. Repeat this pattern 25 times.

3. Add a further 7 silver beads and a crimp. Bring the beading wire through the ring of the other side of the clasp and back through the crimp. Tighten the necklace so that there are no spaces between the beads, close the crimp, and snip off any remaining beading wire. Add the crimp covers.

WATERMELON SLICES NECKLACE

ALTHOUGH MANY GEMSTONES ARE VALUED FOR THEIR
CONSISTENCY AND REGULARITY, SOME ARE TREASURED FOR
THE VERY OPPOSITE. "WATERMELON" TOURMALINE IS ONE OF
THE MOST BEAUTIFUL OF THE LATTER. TOURMALINE CAN COME
IN MANY DIFFERENT COLORS, AND OCCASIONALLY CRYSTALS ARE
FOUND WITH A CORE OF ONE COLOR AND AN OUTER LAYER OF
ANOTHER. WHEN THESE CRYSTALS ARE SLICED, THE BEAUTIFUL
PATTERN IS DISPLAYED TO ITS GREATEST ADVANTAGE. OFTEN,
THE SLICES HAVE A PINK INTERIOR AND GREEN "SKIN" THAT IS
REMINISCENT OF A SLICED WATERMELON. INCREASINGLY DIFFICULT
TO FIND, GOOD WATERMELON TOURMALINE IS SOMETHING TO
ACQUIRE WHEN YOU SEE IT. IN SMALL SIZES, THE PURPLE TONES
OF AMETHYST BECOME MORE SUBDUED, MAKING THEM GOOD
SPACERS TO SHOW OFF THE TOURMALINE.

1. Thread a crimp on the beading wire. Pass the wire through the ring of one half of the clasp and back through the crimp. Make sure that the beading wire is tight around the ring and squeeze the crimp shut. Thread on a 3mm silver bead so that it fits over the tail of the wire and cut off any excess wire.

2. Thread on three 2mm amethyst beads and a tourmaline slice.

3. Add five 2mm amethyst beads and a tourmaline slice. Repeat this pattern 8 times. Add three 2mm amethyst beads, a tourmaline bead, and 3 more amethyst beads. Reverse and repeat the 5 amethyst bead and 1 tourmaline pattern from this step 10 times, to mirror the first half of the necklace.

4. Now add three 2mm amethyst beads and the other 3mm silver bead and a crimp. Bring the beading wire through the ring of the other side of the clasp and back through the crimp and the first round silver bead. Tighten the necklace so that all the beads are snugly together, close the crimp, and snip off any remaining beading wire. Add the crimp covers.

5. Add the final tourmaline slice to the headpin and make a wire-wrapped loop. Use the jump ring to attach this pendant to the last ring of the clasp.

TOOLS
Wire Cutters, Crimping Pliers

MATERIALS (FOR A 20" NECKLACE)
- 22 10mm to 12mm side-drilled slices of watermelon tourmaline
- 102 2mm amethyst round beads
- 2 3mm hollow seamless silver round beads
- 1 5mm silver jump ring
- 1 ³/₄" silver headpin
- 1 silver toggle extension clasp
- 2 silver crimp beads
- 2 silver crimp bead covers
- 20" of beading wire

NOTE:
The use of an extension clasp allows you to adjust the necklace length, by up to an inch, when you wear it.

CITRINE, GARNET, AND CHAIN NECKLACE

THESE BEAUTIFUL CITRINE DROPS, CUT IN AN UNUSUAL TWISTED SHAPE, ARE SUCH A STRONG FOCAL POINT OF THE DESIGN THAT SIMPLE CHAIN SERVES WELL FOR MUCH OF THE LENGTH OF THE NECKLACE. CHAIN USED IN THIS MANNER ALSO OFFERS A PLEASANT ECONOMY, REDUCING THE NEED FOR MORE GEMS.

1. Arrange the citrine drops in matching pairs on either side of the largest central bead so that they decline in size as they retreat from the center. Twisted drops are likely to be a little irregular, so do not bother trying to match them exactly; there only needs to be a rough graduation, allowing the central bead to be the focus.

2. Thread a crimp on the beading wire. Pass the wire through the end link of one of the pieces of chain and back through the crimp. Make sure that the beading wire is tight around the link and squeeze the crimp shut. Add a 2mm round gold bead so that it covers the tail of the wire and cut away any excess.

3. Add 5 garnet beads and another gold bead. Starting at the end of the line of citrine beads add 1 of the drops to the wire followed by another gold bead.

4. Add 3 garnet beads, a gold bead, the next citrine drop, and a gold bead. Repeat this pattern 7 more times. Then add the last 5 garnet beads and a gold bead.

5. Add a crimp. Bring the beading wire through the end link of the other piece of chain and back through the crimp and the last 2 gold beads. Tighten the necklace so that there are no spaces between the beads, close the crimp, and snip off any remaining beading wire. Add the crimp covers.

6. Use the jump ring to attach the gold ring to one of the ends of the chain. Open the ring of the lobster clasp and attach it to the other end of the chain.

TOOLS
Wire Cutters, Crimping Pliers, Flat-Nosed Pliers

MATERIALS
9 citrine faceted twisted drops ranging in size from 9mm by 13.5mm to 15mm by 17mm

34 1.5mm faceted round garnet beads

20 2mm hollow gold-filled round beads

2 4½" pieces of cable chain with 5mm links

1 gold-filled lobster clasp

1 6mm gold-filled ring

1 4mm gold-filled jump ring

2 gold-filled crimp beads

2 gold-filled crimp bead covers

7" of beading wire

EARRINGS

GOLD FOIL LAMPWORK GLASS EARRINGS

(PICTURED ON OPPOSING PAGE, TOP)

A SIMPLER VARIATION OF THESE EARRINGS CAN BE CREATED REPLACING THE DANGLES WITH A SINGLE CRYSTAL BEAD ABOVE THE LAMPWORK BEAD.

1. To a headpin add a 3mm round bead, a daisy, a glass bead and another daisy and 3mm bead. Cut the headpin ⅝" from the last bead and make a wire-wrapped loop (see Jewelry Techniques).

2. Add a crystal bead and a 2.5mm round bead to the stem of an earwire and make a simple half finished loop. Attach it to the wire-wrapped loop and close it to finish the earring.

TOOLS
Wire Cutters, Round Nose and Flat Nose Pliers

MATERIALS

- 2   20mm by 13mm Czech lampwork glass beads with gold foil.
- 2   4mm Swarovski crystal aurum bi-cone beads (5301)
- 4   4mm vermeil daisy spacer beads
- 2   2.5mm gold-filled hollow seamless round beads
- 4   3mm gold-filled hollow seamless round beads
- 2   2" gold-filled headpins with ball
- 2   gold-filled "add-on" earwires

LAMPWORK GLASS AND CRYSTAL DANGLE EARRINGS

(PICTURED ON OPPOSING PAGE, BOTTOM)

THESE LOVELY GLASS BEADS, WHICH USE TRADITIONAL EUROPEAN-STYLE GLASS TECHNIQUES TO CREATE CONTEMPORARY STYLE, ARE WRAPPED WITH GOLD FOIL. ALTHOUGH MOST SILVER AND GOLD FOIL BEADS ENCASE THE FOIL IN A LAYER OF GLASS, THIS GOLD SITS ON THE SURFACE AND APPEARS JUST AS RICH AS SOLID GOLD. BECAUSE IT IS PURE GOLD, IT WILL NOT TARNISH, AND BECAUSE IT IS FUSED TO THE MOLTEN GLASS DURING PRODUCTION, THE BOND IS PERMANENT. THE OUTSIDE GLASS SWIRL IS RAISED ABOVE THE LEVEL OF THE GOLD AND PROTECTS IT FROM ANY EXCESSIVE RUBBING.

1. To an eyepin, add a 2.5mm round bead, a daisy spacer bead, a glass bead, and another daisy spacer bead. Cut the eyepin ⅝" from the last bead and begin a wire-wrapped loop (page 23). Attach to the earwire and complete the wrapping of the loop.

TOOLS
Wire Cutters, Round-Nosed Pliers,

Flat-Nosed Pliers

MATERIALS

- 2   2" gold-filled eyepins
- 2   2.5mm gold-filled hollow seamless round beads
- 4   4mm vermeil daisy spacer beads
- 2   gold-filled earwires
- 2   20mm by 13mm Czech lampwork glass beads with gold foil
- 6   4mm Swarovski crystal aurum bi-cone beads (5301)
- 6   2mm gold-filled hollow seamless round beads
- 6   ½" gold-filled headpins with ball tips
- 2   3.5mm gold-filled rings

2. To make the dangles, add a crystal bead and a 2mm round bead to a headpin. Make a simple half-finished loop. Attach it to a ring and finish closing the loop. Make and attach two more of these dangles to the ring.

3. Open the loop of the eyepin, attach the ring with the three dangles, and re-close the loop.

THAI SILVER AND HANDMADE GLASS EARRINGS

(PICTURED ON PAGE 142, CENTER)

THE SILVER FOIL EMBEDDED IN THESE HANDMADE GLASS BEADS COUPLED WITH THE "BEAN" BEAD CREATES A THICK CENTRAL SILVER CORE FOR THE SOFT VIOLET HUES OF THE GLASS "WINGS."

1. Start the earring by adding a silver round bead to your headpin. Add a silver foil lamp bead, a "bean" bead, an d another round bead. Start making the beginning of a wire wrapped loop (see Jewelry Techniques).

2. Slip the loop onto the ring of the earwire and wrap the tail of the headpin around the base of the loop. Note: Make sure that "bean" bead sits so the decorated ends are perpendicular to the wings of the glass bead.

TOOLS
Wire Cutters, Round-Nosed Pliers,
Flat-Nosed Pliers and Cutters

MATERIALS
2   10 by 15mm silver foil lamp beads
2   5 by 10mm Thai silver "bean" shape beads
4   2.5mm silver seamless hollow round beads
2   2 inch sterling silver head pins with a tri-dot decoration
1   pair sterling silver earwires

NOTE
Before starting this pair of earrings, you will need to read how to make a wire wrapped loop in the Techniques section.

CRYSTAL BARBELL AND SILVER CHAIN EARRINGS

(PICTURED ON PAGE 147, TOP LEFT)

THIS NEW SHAPE FROM SWAROVSKI IS LIKE A TINY FACETED BARBELL. THE "ADD-ON" EARWIRES ALLOW FOR EASY EMBELLISHMENT.

1. Add three crystal beads and a 3mm silver bead to a 1" headpin. Make sure the crystal beads are tightly seated on each other. Start a wire-wrapped loop, but before wrapping, hook on to it one of the pieces of chain.

2. Add a 2mm silver bead, a crystal bead, and another 2mm bead to the "add-on" earwire; make a simple loop. Open the loop, attach it to the other end of the chain, and close.

TOOLS
Round-Nosed Pliers, Flat-Nosed Pliers, Wire Cutters

MATERIALS
8 11mm x 5mm Swarovski "barbell" crystal beads

2 3mm seamless hollow silver round beads

4 2mm hollow silver round beads

2 1" silver headpins with ball tip

2 1" pieces of silver cable chain with 3.5mm links

2 silver "add-on" earwires

DICHROIC GLASS EARRINGS

(PICTURED ON PAGE 147, BOTTOM)

WHEN THE GLASS IS AS STUNNING AS THESE DICHROIC SQUARES BY SCOTT TURNBALL, IT REQUIRES ONLY THE SIMPLEST OF SETTINGS TO BECOME DAZZLING EARRINGS. HERE THE JET BLACK ONYX BEADS MATCH THE UNDERLYING COLOR OF THE MAIN BEAD.

1. Add a gold-filled bead, a dichroic bead, another gold-filled bead, a black onyx bead, and another gold-filled bead to a headpin. Cut the headpin at least ¼" above the round bead, and make a simple loop.

2. Slip the loop onto the loop of the earwire and close.

TOOLS
Round-Nosed Pliers, Flat-Nosed Pliers, Wire Cutters

MATERIALS
2 11mm flat square dichroic glass beads

2 4mm faceted round black onyx beads

6 3mm gold-filled seamless hollow round beads

2 1½" gold-filled headpins with ball tip

2 gold-filled earwires

DICHROIC GLASS WITH GOLD AND PERIDOT EARRINGS

(PICTURED ON OPPOSING PAGE, TOP RIGHT)

AN UNDERLYING CORE OF GREEN GLASS FLASHES THROUGH THE BRIGHT BRONZE OF THE DICHROIC FIRE IN THESE BEADS INSPIRED BY THE ADDITION OF PALE GREEN PERIDOT DANGLES.

1. Add a faceted bead, a dichroic bead, another faceted bead, a peridot bead, and a final faceted bead to a 1" headpin. Make a simple loop.

2. Add a faceted bead, a peridot bead, a daisy spacer bead, another peridot bead, and a faceted bead to another 1" headpin. Cut the headpin leaving ¼" and make a simple loop.

3. Add a faceted bead, three daisy spacer beads, and another faceted bead to a third 1" headpin. Cut the headpin leaving ¼" and make a simple loop.

4. Open a jump ring. Pass it through the loops of the three headpins, the loop of the earwire, and close.

TOOLS
Round-Nosed Pliers, Flat-Nosed Pliers, Wire Cutters

MATERIALS
2   10mm rondel dichroic glass beads
6   3.5mm round peridot beads
8   4mm vermeil daisy spacer beads
14   2.1mm gold-filled hollow faceted beads
6   1" gold-filled headpins
2   3.5mm gold-filled jump rings
2   vermeil decorated earwires

VERMEIL AND TOURMALINE EARRINGS

(PICTURED ON OPPOSING PAGE, BOTTOM)

EARRINGS ARE EASY TO DESIGN AND QUICK TO CONSTRUCT. EVEN WITH ONLY A FEW MINUTES TO SPARE, I CAN THROW TOGETHER A PAIR OF EARRINGS TO MATCH THE DRESS I AM ABOUT TO WEAR THAT EVENING. I LET MY EYES PASS OVER THE BITS AND PIECES OF JEWELRY COMPONENTS THAT LITTER THE FLAT SURFACES OF MY STUDIO AND SELECT A FEW BEADS. IN A COUPLE OF MOMENTS, I HAVE THEM ON A HEADPIN: I MAKE A LOOP, ATTACH AN EARWIRE, AND HOLD UP A PERFECTLY FINISHED PIECE OF JEWELRY. OF COURSE, EARRINGS ARE SOMETIMES FAR MORE COMPLEX AND REQUIRE A GREAT DEAL MORE TIME TO CONSTRUCT, BUT IN GENERAL, THEY ARE THE QUICKEST ROUTE TO INSTANT GRATIFICATION.

TOOLS

Beading Needle, Awl, Scissors, Flat-Nosed Pliers, Hypo-Cement or Clear Nail Polish

MATERIALS

18 inches of #83 turquoise silk thread, size F

2 gold-filled basket bead tips

1 pair of gold-filled earwires

6 3mm gold-filled seamless hollow round beads

2 12mm vermeil hollow round beads with perforated star pattern

26 green tourmaline sticks approx. 3mm wide and 5mm to 10mm long (A 16" strand will leave enough extra sticks for a pair of earrings)

1. Read the instructions in Jewelry Techniques for stringing on silk thread and basket bead tips. Thread a beading needle with nine inches of the thread. Double it and make a knot at the end of the doubled thread. Following the instructions in Jewelry Techniques (page 20), add one of the basket bead tips. Attach it to an earwire. Add a dab of hypo-cement (or clear nail polish) to the knot on the outside of the bead tip. Cut off the tail of the thread very close to the knot.

2. Add a 3mm round bead, then a 12mm vermeil bead. Now add twelve of the green tourmaline sticks and check that the earring is the right length for you. Add or subtract sticks to adjust the length, taking care that you have enough beads left over to make the other earring the same length as the first. Make a knot and use your awl to make sure that the knot is tight against the beads. Add a small dab of cement.

3. Complete the second earring as above, laying it against the other before the final knot and adjusting the number of tourmaline sticks to equalize the lengths.

GOLD AND CRYSTAL EARRINGS

(PICTURED ON PAGE 149, TOP)

ANOTHER EXAMPLE OF HOW WELL FINE GLASS CAN GO WITH
VERMEIL, PARTICULARLY WHEN IT IS A COLOR WHICH SO SUBTLY
ENHANCES THE GOLDEN HUE OF THE OTHER 2 BEADS.

1. Start the earring by making all the little crystal dangles. Add to each ¹/₂" headpin a crystal and a 2mm gold bead. Make a simple loop (see Jewelry Techniques, page 23).

2. To each earwire, add one of the remaining crystal beads and a 3mm gold bead, then make a simple loop.

3. To each 2" headpin, add a 2.5mm gold bead, a 9mm gold bead, another 2.5mm bead, nine dangles, and a 3mm bead. Cut the headpin about ⁵/₈" above the last bead and make a wire-wrapped loop (see Jewelry Techniques, page 23). Attach this to the earwire by opening the loop of the earwire.

TOOLS
Round-Nosed Pliers, Flat-Nosed Pliers,
Wire Cutters

MATERIALS

18	¹/₂" vermeil headpins with ball tips
20	4.5mm Swarovski 5310 (simplicity) crystal Golden Shadow beads
18	2mm gold-filled seamless hollow round beads
1	pair gold-filled "add-on" earwires
2	3mm gold-filled seamless hollow round beads
2	2" vermeil headpins with ball tips
4	2.5mm gold-filled seamless hollow round beads
2	9mm gold-filled seamless hollow round beads

POTATO PEARL AND CHAIN EARRINGS (PICTURED ON PAGE 152, TOP)

ANOTHER ENCHANTING ASPECT OF EARRINGS IS THE OPPORTUNITY THEY GIVE YOU TO USE ALL THE ODDS AND ENDS THAT REMAIN AFTER DESIGNING A NECKLACE. THERE ARE ALWAYS A FEW BEADS LEFT; WHY NOT USE THEM TO MAKE A SET OF MATCHING PEARL EARRINGS?

1. Make the dangles by adding 1 gold bead, 1 pearl, and 1 gold bead to a headpin (see "Using Headpins and Eyepins," page 22). Finish by making a loop. Make 30 of these in a mixture of colors.

2. Cut 2 pieces from the long-and-short chain so that each has 4 long links surrounding 3 short links. They should each be about 1½ inch long.

3. Slip an earwire through an end loop of the chain so that it hangs from the loop.

4. Open a jump ring, and add 3 of the dangles. Hook the ring onto the other end of the chain and close.

5. Using 3 more jump rings, attach 3 dangles to each of the 3 short links in the chain. Make sure you add the jump rings to the same side of the chain each time.

6. Add 3 more dangles to a jump ring and attach to the loop of the earwire.

TOOLS
Wire Cutters, Round-Nosed Pliers, Flat-Nosed Pliers

MATERIALS

30 5mm potato-shaped pearls in various dyed colors (about a third of a 16" multicolor strand)

60 2.5mm gold-filled round beads

4 inches of gold-filled "long-and-short" chain (with long links measuring about ⁵/₁₆")

10 4mm gold-filled jump rings

30 ½" gold-filled headpins with ball tip

2 vermeil earwires

ROUND PEARL AND CHAIN EARRINGS

(PICTURED ON OPPOSING PAGE, CENTER)

THE CHAIN USED IN THIS DESIGN IS CALLED "LONG AND SHORT" BECAUSE IT ALTERNATES ONE LONG LINK WITH ONE SHORT LINK.

1. Cut the chain into two 1-inch pieces, two 1 ½-inch pieces, and two 2-inch pieces.

2. Make the pearl pendants by adding 1 gold bead, 1 pearl, and 1 gold bead to a headpin and forming a loop (see "Using Headpins and Eyepins," page 22). Make 6 of these.

3. Open the loop of a pendant and attach it to the end of a 2-inch chain. Add another pendant to the end of a 1½-inch chain. Add another to the end of a 1-inch chain.

4. Open the loop of the earwire, and add the pendants by attaching the end link of the chain. Start with the 1½-inch chain, followed by the 2-inch chain and then the 1-inch chain.

TOOLS

Round-Nosed Pliers, Flat-Nosed Pliers

MATERIALS

30 3mm round pearls in natural silver tones

30 2.5mm sterling silver round beads

4" sterling silver long-and-short chain (with long links measuring about $5/16$")

10 3mm sterling silver jump rings

30 ½" sterling silver headpins with ball tip

COIN PEARL AND CHAIN EARRINGS (PICTURED ON OPPOSING PAGE, BOTTOM)

1. Make the dangles by adding a pearl and silver bead to a headpin (see "Using Headpins and Eyepins," page 22), and then making a loop. Make 30 of these.

2. To complete and finish the earrings, follow the instructions in steps 2–6 for "Potato Pearl and Chain earrings" (page 151).

MATERIALS

6   10mm white coin pearls

9" gold-filled fine cable chain (with links measuring about 3mm)

12 5mm gold-filled round beads

6   1" mm gold-filled headpins with ball tip

2   gold-filled earwires with ball

"STARDUST" AND CHAIN EARRINGS (PICTURED ON OPPOSING PAGE, TOP)

STARDUST IS THE NAME OF A CERTAIN TYPE OF SILVER FINISH. THE PLAIN SURFACE IS COATED WITH HUNDREDS OF TINY GRAINS OF SILVER THAT TWINKLE LIKE LITTLE STARS.

1. Cut the chain into two sections, each containing six rings. To one end of each attach two stardust balls by opening their loops. On the third ring, add another. On the fourth ring, add another. On the last ring, add one more.

2. Make the CZ dangles by adding one CZ bead to each of the headpins and making a simple loop. Attach one of these beside each single stardust ball, making sure to use three of each color in the same order on each earring.

3. Open the loops of the earwires and attach them to the fourth rings (from the two silver balls) of each piece of chain, making sure that you have used the same ring on each piece of the chain.

TOOLS

Flat-Nosed Pliers, Wire Cutters

MATERIALS

4" of silver chain with 10mm rings

10 4mm silver "stardust" balls with loops

6 4mm cubic zirconia (CZ) faceted round beads in three colors (two each in lime, pink, and purple)

6 $\frac{1}{2}$" silver headpins with ball tip

1 pair of silver earwires with green CZ

SILVER CHAIN AND CRYSTAL EARRINGS (PICTURED ON OPPOSING PAGE, BOTTOM)

A FEW LINKS OF PRECIOUS METAL CHAIN CAN MAKE BEAUTIFUL EARRINGS, ESPECIALLY WHEN PAIRED WITH A SINGLE DRAMATIC BEAD. ADJUST THE NUMBER OF LINKS TO CREATE A LENGTH THAT FLATTERS YOUR NECK.

1. Cut the chain into two 2" sections. To one end of each attach the crystal bead using the 8mm jump ring.

2. To the other end attach the earwire by opening its loop and closing it around the last link of the chain.

TOOLS

Flat-Nosed Pliers, Wire Cutters

MATERIALS

4" of silver chain 15mm textured links joined by 7mm plain round links

2 22mm top-drilled Swarovski crystal aquamarine 6015 "polygon" beads

2 8mm silver jump rings

1 pair of silver earwires with blue cubic zirconia (CZ)

HORIZONTAL STICK PEARL EARRINGS (PICTURED ON OPPOSING PAGE, CENTER)

THE SIZE OF A SINGLE PEARL IS JUST ABOUT AS BIG AS YOU WANT AN EARRING TO BE, SO STICK PEARLS ARE GREAT CHOICES.

1. Start by making the 6 dangles. Add to a headpin one spacer, a zircon, and another spacer, and then make a loop.

2. Put a stick pearl on a headpin, and make a loop at the end without the ball tip. Turn it so that the pearl is sitting on the loop. Now make a semi-finished loop at the top. Slip it through the loop of the earwire, and wrap the tail of the headpin under the loop so that the little ball at the tip comes to rest at the top of the pearl. (In this way, the gold ball creates a little drop of gold on the pearl, forming an integral part of the design.)

3. Open the jump ring, and use it to attach three dangles to the bottom loop of the headpin.

TOOLS
Wire Cutters, Round-Nosed Pliers, Flat-Nosed Pliers

MATERIALS
- 2 20mm stick pearls
- 6 4mm faceted natural zircon rondels
- 12 3mm vermeil daisy spacer beads
- 2 3mm gold-filled ring
- 8 $1/2$" gold-filled headpins with ball tip
- 2 vermeil earwires with decoration

VERTICAL STICK PEARL EARRINGS (PICTURED ON OPPOSING PAGE, BOTTOM)

1. Cut the long headpin about $5/8$" longer than the pearl. Put it through the pearl and make a loop at the end without the ball. Following step 2 for the Horizontal Stick Pearl Earrings (above), let the pearl rest on the loop and create another at the top to attach the earwire. Twist the tail of the wire so the ball rests at top of the pearl.

2. To a headpin, add 1 bead cap, 1 pearl, 1 bead cap, and 1 round bead. Make a loop and attach to the bottom loop of the stick pearl.

TOOLS
Wire Cutters, Round-Nosed Pliers, Flat-Nosed Pliers

MATERIALS
- 2 20mm stick pearls
- 2 7mm coral beads
- 2 2.5mm gold-filled round beads
- 4 5mm vermeil bead caps
- 2 3mm gold-filled rings
- 2 $1/2$" and two $11/2$" gold-filled headpins with ball tip
- 2 gold-filled earwires with decoration

CHANDELIER EARRINGS

(PICTURED ON PAGE 157, TOP)

THIS DESIGN USES A SPECIALTY FINDING FOR CHANDELIER
EARRINGS. THE FIVE LOOPS AT THE BOTTOM CREATE THE
CHANDELIER EFFECT CAUSED BY THE HANGING PEARLS.

1. Cut the wire into 28 1-inch pieces.

2. Using a piece of wire, make a wire-wrapped loop and add a
    pearl. Make an unfinished loop at the other end of the wire.
    Attach it to the outside loop of the chandelier earring finding
    and finish the loop by wrapping. You will need very narrow-
    nosed flat pliers to finish the wrapping.

3. Attach another 4 pearls to the other chandelier loops in the same
    way.

4. Attach another pearl to each of the previous rows of pearls,
    using the wire pieces and the same wire-wrapping technique.

5. Attach another pearl to the middle three rows in the same
    manner.

6. Attach another pearl to the middle row in the same manner.

7. Attach a final pearl to each row by adding it to a headpin and
    making a wire-wrapped loop.

8. Add another pearl to a headpin and attach it to the inside loop of
    the chandelier earring finding.

TOOLS
Wire Cutters, Round-Nosed Pliers,
Flat-Nosed Pliers

MATERIALS
40   3mm white potato-shaped pearls

 2   16–27mm vermeil chandelier earring
findings

12   ¹/₂" vermeil headpins with ball tip

28" 26-gauge gold-filled wire

 2   gold-filled earwires with ball

GOLD AND CRYSTAL HOLIDAY SPARKLE EARRINGS

(PICTURED ON PAGE 160, CENTER)

SPACER BARS, WHEN THEY ARE LINKED TOGETHER WITH JUMP RINGS, CAN CREATE A CHAIN-LIKE EFFECT.

1. Start the earring by making all the little crystal dangles. Add a 1.5mm gold charlotte bead, a crystal, and another 1.5mm gold bead to each $1/2$" headpin; make a simple loop.

2. Open the jump rings. Add three dangles to a jump ring and then hook it to one ring of the chain. Close the jump ring. Repeat this to add three dangles to each of the other rings.

3. Open the loop of the earwire and add the end of the chain. Add three dangles to a jump ring and close. Add that jump ring to the open earwire loop and then close.

TOOLS
Round-Nose Pliers, Flat-Nose Pliers

MATERIALS

24	3mm bicone Swarovski crystal beads with 2xAB coating
48	size $11/0$ gold-plated charlotte seed beads
2	$11/8$" pieces of gold-filled "long and short" chain, each with 3 long bars and 3 rings
8	3mm gold-filled jump rings
24	$1/2$" gold-filled headpins with ball tip
1	pair gold-filled earwires

SILVER AND CRYSTAL HOOP EARRINGS (PICTURED ON OPPOSING PAGE, TOP)

USING HOOP EARWIRES IS ONE OF THE SIMPLEST WAYS TO MAKE EARRINGS—JUST ADD A FEW CRYSTALS, AND THEY ARE GOOD TO GO. THESE CRYSTAL DROPS ARE JUST AS EASY TO USE AS ROUNDS BUT GIVE A LITTLE EXTRA DIMENSION TO THE DESIGN.

1. Add a round silver bead and then a crystal drop to the hoop. Repeat twelve times and add a final silver bead.

2. Use the flat-nosed piers to bend ¼" of the straight end of the hoop wire into a right angle so it will catch in the looped end to close the earring.

TOOLS
Flat-Nosed Pliers

MATERIALS

26	6mm x 4mm Swarovski crystal top-drilled drops
28	2mm hollow silver round beads
2	1" silver hoop earwires

CRYSTAL AND VERMEIL EARRINGS

(PICTURED ON OPPOSING PAGE, BOTTOM)

VERMEIL IS A WONDERFUL MATERIAL, MUCH LESS EXPENSIVE THAN GOLD BUT AS VALUABLE AND DURABLE AS PRECIOUS METAL. FOR THESE EARRINGS, THE EARWIRE, OR STUD, IS AS MUCH A PART OF THE DESIGN AS THE CRYSTAL. THE LARGE ROUND GOLDEN SHAPE COUNTERBALANCES THE LARGER OF THE CRYSTAL BEADS.

1. Add an 8mm crystal bead, a bead cap with its convex side facing the bead, a 4mm crystal, and a 2mm gold bead to a headpin.

2. Make a simple loop above the last bead. Open the loop, attach it to the ring of the ear stud, and then close.

TOOLS
Round-Nosed Pliers, Flat-Nosed Pliers

MATERIALS

2	8mm round Swarovski crystal beads
2	4mm bicone Swarovski crystal beads
2	5mm Bali-style vermeil bead caps
2	2mm hollow gold-filled round beads
2	1" gold-filled headpins
2	vermeil ear studs with 8mm diameter faces

FAUX PEARL AND CHAIN EARRINGS (PICTURED ON OPPOSING PAGE, TOP)

CONSIDERING THE IMMENSE SATISFACTION IT BRINGS, THIS DESIGN SEEMS ALMOST CRIMINALLY SIMPLE . OF COURSE, EARRINGS ARE SOMETIMES FAR MORE COMPLEX THAN THESE AND CAN TAKE MORE TIME , BUT OF ALL THE TYPES OF JEWELRY, THEY OFFER THE QUICKEST ROUTE TO INSTANT GRATIFICATION.

TO A HEADPIN (SEE "USING HEADPINS AND EYEPINS," PAGE 22), ADD 1 FAUX PEARL, AND THEN MAKE A SIMPLE LOOP TO ATTACH IT TO THE END LINK OF A PIECE OF THE CHAIN. ATTACH THE EARWIRE TO THE OTHER END LINK OF THE CHAIN.

TOOLS
Round-Nosed Pliers, Flat-Nosed Pliers

MATERIALS
- 2 12mm faux pearls
- 2 ½" pieces of gold-filled cable chain with 6-mm links
- 2 1" gold-filled headpins
- 2 vermeil earwires

TAHITIAN PEARL EARRINGS

(PICTURED ON OPPOSING PAGE, CENTER)

WHEN PAIRED SIMPLY WITH A LITTLE HEADDRESS OF SOLID GOLD TO FORM A DROP SHAPE, THESE LOVELY EXAMPLES OF THE TAHITIAN "BLACK" PEARL WORK PERFECTLY.

TO A HEADPIN (SEE "USING HEADPINS AND EYEPINS," PAGE 22), ADD 1 PEARL, 1 BEAD CAP, AND 1 ROUND BEAD. MAKE A LOOP AND ATTACH IT TO THE EARWIRE. REPEAT, AND YOU HAVE YOUR EARRINGS.

TOOLS
Round-Nosed Pliers, Flat-Nosed Pliers

MATERIALS
- 2 10mm baroque Tahitian black pearls
- 2 6mm 18K gold bead caps
- 2 1" gold-filled headpins
- 2 2mm 18K gold round beads
- 2 18K gold earwires with decoration

MOTHER-OF-PEARL EARRINGS

(PICTURED ON PAGE 163, BOTTOM)

THIS RICH, IRIDESCENT MOTHER-OF-PEARL COMES FROM THE
INSIDE OF ABALONE SHELLS. THESE LARGE COMPOSITE BEADS
ARE CREATED BY CUTTING THE MOTHER-OF-PEARL NACRE INTO
SMALL PIECES TO FORM A MOSAIC. THUS, YOU ENJOY A LARGE
AREA OF THE ABALONE PEARL'S PEACOCK BLUES AND GREENS.
EARRINGS ARE EASY TO DESIGN AND QUICK TO CONSTRUCT. IN
ONLY A FEW MINUTES, IT'S POSSIBLE TO THROW TOGETHER A
PAIR OF EARRINGS TO MATCH THE DRESS YOU PLAN TO WEAR
THAT EVENING. SELECT A FEW BEADS, PUT THEM ON A HEADPIN,
MAKE A LOOP, ATTACH AN EARWIRE, AND HOLD UP A PERFECTLY
FINISHED PIECE OF JEWELRY.

1. To an eyepin (see "Using Headpins and Eyepins," page 22), add 1
    gold bead, 1 mother-of pearl bead, and 1 gold bead. Make a
    wire-wrapped loop (as described in "Wire Wrapping," page 23)
    and attach to the earwire.

2. Add a round pearl to a headpin and make a half-finished loop.
    Attach it to the eye of the eyepin and wrap to finish closing the
    loop. Make and attach 3 of these to each earring.

TOOLS
Round-Nosed Pliers, Flat-Nosed Pliers

MATERIALS

2   17 by 13mm composite abalone
    mother-of -pearl beads

6   4mm round white freshwater pearls

2   2" gold-filled eyepins

6   ½" gold-filled headpins with
    ball tip

4   2.5mm gold-filled round beads

2   vermeil earwires

EYEPINS
An eyepin is just a headpin with a loop at the
bottom instead of a flattened tip. If you do not
have an eyepin available, simply take a headpin,
cut off the flattened tip, and use your round-
nosed pliers to make a small loop. It will be
slightly shorter than the headpin but should
work nicely. If you don't have a headpin, try
making your eyepins using the same method on
a simple piece of wire. Just cut a couple of
2-inch segments, and form small loops at one
end.

GOLD AND PREHNITE EARRINGS (PICTURED ON PAGE 166, TOP)

GOLD AND A BEAUTIFUL GEMSTONE—SOMETIMES, ABSOLUTE
SIMPLICITY IS THE WAY TO GO!

1. Start the earring by adding a bead cap to your headpin. Add the
   prehnite oval nugget, another bead cap, and the 2.5mm round
   gold bead, and start making the beginning of a wire wrapped
   loop (see Jewelry Techniques).

2. Slip the loop onto the ring of the earwire and wrap the tail of the
   headpin around the base of the loop.

TOOLS
Round-Nosed Pliers

MATERIALS
4   2.5mm 18 karat gold bead caps

2   1" 18 karat headpins with ball tip

2   10mm by 13mm prehnite smooth
    oval nuggets

2   2.5mm 18 karat gold round beads

1   pair 18 karat gold earwires

PEARL AND CORAL EARRINGS

(PICTURED ON PAGE 166, BOTTOM)

THESE WONDERFUL DOUBLE-ENDED BEAD CAPS PRESENT AN X
DESIGN ON EACH OF FOUR SIDES. WHEN VIEWED HORIZONTALLY,
THEY LOOK LIKE A LITTLE BOW DECORATING THE BEAUTIFUL
LARGE PEARLS

1. Start the earring by adding a gold-filled cube bead to a headpin.
   Add a pearl, an X-shaped bead cap, a coral bead, another cube
   bead, and then start making the beginning of a wire-wrapped
   loop (see Jewelry Techniques).

2. Slip the loop onto the ring of the earwire and wrap the tail of the
   headpin around the base of the loop.

TOOLS
Round-Nosed Pliers, Flat-Nosed Pliers,
Wire Cutters

MATERIALS
4   2.5mm gold-filled cube beads

2   2" vermeil headpins with ball tip

2   8mm by 12mm rice-shaped freshwater
    pearls

2   6mm by 8mm vermeil X-shaped
    double-ended bead caps

2   5mm coral round beads

1   pair gold-filled earwires

NOTE
Before starting this pair of earrings, you
need to read how to make a wire-wrapped
loop in the Jewelry Techniques section.

GOLD AND TOPAZ EARRINGS

(PICTURED ON OPPOSING PAGE, CENTER)

ALTHOUGH THE AMOUNT OF GOLD IN THE RESERVES OF NATIONAL GOVERNMENTS IS HIGHEST IN THE UNITED STATES AND THE EUROPEAN UNION, INDIA IS FIRST IN OVERALL OWNERSHIP OF GOLD. INDIAN WOMEN PLACE A LOT OF IMPORTANCE ON OWNING GOLD JEWELRY, AND THEY DESIRE EVER-GROWING COLLECTIONS OF NECKLACES, EARRINGS, BROOCHES, AND OTHER ACCESSO-RIES—ALL IN SOLID GOLD OF AT LEAST 22 KARATS. BUT BEFORE GASPING AT SUCH UNRESTRAINED VANITY, UNDERSTAND THAT IN MUCH OF ASIA, GOLD JEWELRY IS VIEWED MORE AS A SAVINGS ACCOUNT THAN A SIMPLE DECORATION. IT CAN BE FREELY EX-CHANGED FOR MONEY AND IS CONSIDERED AS GOOD AS CASH IN THE BANK. IT DOES NOT EARN ANY INTEREST, BUT THERE IS GREAT FAITH IN ITS ABILITY TO MAINTAIN ITS VALUE AND APPRECIATE OVER TIME.

TOOLS
Round-Nosed Pliers, Flat-Nosed Pliers, Wire Cutters

MATERIALS
- 2 1" 18 karat gold headpins with ball tip
- 12 2mm 18 karat gold faceted beads
- 2 3mm faceted disc-shaped London blue topaz beads
- 1 pair of 18 karat gold earwires
- 8 ½" 18 karat gold headpins with ball tip

1. To each 1-inch headpin, add a gold faceted bead, a topaz bead, and another gold faceted bead. Make the beginnings of a wire-wrapped loop (see page 23). Attach this to the earwire and finish wrapping the tail of the headpin around the base of the loop.

2. To make the little dangles, add a faceted gold bead to each half-inch headpin. Make a simple loop and add another 2mm gold bead. Make a simple loop, and before closing, attach the dangle to the loop of the earwire. Add four of these dangles to each earwire.

CLOCKWISE FROM TOP: Larimar Earrings; Serpentine, Carnelian, and Citrine Earrings;
Lapis Lazuli and Coral Earrings; Black Onyx and Gold Earrings; Precious Beryl Earrings

LARIMAR EARRINGS

(PICTURED ON OPPOSING PAGE, TOP)

THE EFFECT OF A BEAD CAP CAN SOMETIMES BE CREATED BY USING A DIFFERENT KIND OF BEAD. THESE HOLLOW GOLD BEADS SIT ON TOP OF THE LARIMAR WITHOUT EMBRACING IT, YET GIVE THE IMPRESSION OF A GOLDEN CROWN.

1. To each of the headpins add a daisy spacer, a larimar bead, an 18 karat gold disc, and a round gold bead. Begin a simple or a wrapped loop.

2. Slip the unfinished loop over the ring of the ear stud and close it by wire-wrapping.

TOOLS
Round-Nosed Pliers, Flat-Nosed Pliers

MATERIALS

- 2   9mm round larimar beads
- 2   4mm by 7mm puffed-disc 18 karat gold beads
- 2   2mm 18 karat gold daisy spacer beads
- 2   2mm hollow gold round beads
- 2   1" 18 karat gold headpins with ball tip
- 1   pair of 18 karat gold ear studs

SERPENTINE, CARNELIAN, AND CITRINE EARRINGS

(PICTURED ON OPPOSING PAGE, CENTER RIGHT)

HAVING A SLIGHTLY CREEPY NAME AND LOOKING SIMILAR TO JADE, IT IS HARDLY SURPRISING THAT SERPENTINE HAS SEVERAL OTHER, MORE ATTRACTIVE TRADE NAMES LIKE "SOO CHOW JADE" AND "NEW JADE." SOFTER AND LESS EXPENSIVE THAN REAL JADE, IT IS OFTEN FOUND IN CARVED SHAPES, SUCH AS THESE LEAVES.

1. To each 2" headpin add a 3mm gold bead, a serpentine leaf, a vermeil daisy spacer, a carnelian disc, another vermeil daisy spacer, 2 citrine beads, a daisy spacer, and a gold round bead.

2. Make a wire-wrapped loop. Open the loops of the earwires and attach the headpin loops.

TOOLS
Round-Nosed Pliers, Flat-Nosed Pliers, Wire Cutters

MATERIALS

- 2   20mm by 15mm serpentine carved leaf beads
- 2   10mm carnelian disc beads
- 4   5mm faceted rondel citrine beads
- 6   4mm vermeil daisy spacer beads
- 4   3mm seamless hollow gold-filled round beads
- 2   2" vermeil headpins with ball tip
- 1   pair of vermeil earwires

LAPIS LAZULI AND CORAL EARRINGS

(PICTURED ON ON PAGE 168, BOTTOM RIGHT)

BECAUSE OF ITS INCLUSIONS, LAPIS CAN HAVE A SOMEWHAT ORGANIC LOOK AND GOES WELL WITH CORAL.

1. First make the little dangles: add to each ¹/₂" headpin a 3mm coral bead and a 2mm gold bead. Make a simple loop.

2. To each 2" headpin add a 3mm gold bead, a 8mm gold bead, a lapis disc, a 5mm coral bead, 9 dangles, and a 3mm gold bead.

3. Cut the headpin ⁵/₈" above the last bead. Make the beginnings of a wire-wrapped loop. Attach this to the earwire and finish wrapping the tail of the headpin around the base of the loop.

TOOLS
Round-Nosed Pliers, Flat-Nosed Pliers, Wire Cutters

MATERIALS

18	3mm round red coral beads
2	5mm round red coral beads
2	13mm lapis lazuli flat disc beads
18	2mm seamless hollow gold-filled round beads
2	8mm seamless hollow gold-filled round beads
6	3mm seamless hollow gold-filled round beads
18	¹/₂" vermeil headpins with ball tip
2	2" vermeil headpins with ball tip
1	pair of vermeil earwires

BLACK ONYX AND GOLD EARRINGS (PICTURED ON PAGE 168, BOTTOM LEFT)

LIKE A SIMPLE BLACK DRESS, ROUND, MATTE BLACK ONYX BEADS ARE THE MOST MODEST OF FASHIONS, BUT THEY CAN BE THE PERFECT COMPANION FOR THE RICHNESS OF GOLD. THESE ORNA- MENTED VERMEIL BEAD CAPS PROVIDE PLENTY OF GLITTER, BUT THEY NEED THE RESTRAINT OF THE SOBER BLACK ONYX TO BE ELEGANT.

1. Start the earring by making the dangles. Add to each ¹/₂" headpin an onyx bead, a bead cap so that it fits over the onyx bead, and a round gold bead. Make a simple loop.

TOOLS
Round-Nosed Pliers, Flat-Nosed Pliers

MATERIALS

14	4mm round matte black onyx beads
14	6mm vermeil bead caps
2	1¹/₈" pieces of gold-filled "long and short" chain each with 3 long bars and 3 rings
14	2mm hollow gold-filled round beads
6	3.5mm gold-filled jump rings
2	3mm gold-filled jump rings
14	¹/₂" vermeil headpins with ball tip
1	pair gold-filled earwires

2. Open the jump rings. Add 1 dangle to a 3mm jump ring and attach it to the ring at one end of the chain. Close the jump ring. Use a 3.5mm jump ring to add 2 dangles to the next ring of the chain. Repeat this to add another 2 dangles to the next ring of the chain.

3. Attach the end of the chain to the earwire (either by opening the loop of the earwire or slipping it over the hook, depending on the style). Add two dangles to a jump ring and attach it to the loop of the earwire. Close the jump ring.

PRECIOUS BERYL EARRINGS

(PICTURED ON PAGE 168, CENTER LEFT)

A BEAUTIFUL GEMSTONE BEAD REQUIRES LITTLE TO BECOME A STRIKING EARRING. PRECIOUS BERYL IS ALSO KNOWN AS MORGANITE AND PINK AQUAMARINE, BUT THE QUALITY OF THESE BEADS CALLS FOR THE MORE EXPENSIVE-SOUNDING TITLE. GEMS OF THIS QUALITY ARE BEST PAIRED WITH REAL GOLD.

1. To each of the 1½" headpins, add a daisy spacer bead, a precious beryl bead, and another daisy spacer. Cut the headpin about a ¼" above the last bead and make a simple loop.

2. Open the headpin loops to attach them to the loops of the ear studs.

TOOLS
Round-Nosed Pliers, Flat-Nosed Pliers, Wire Cutters

MATERIALS
2 18mm by 12mm lozenge-shaped precious beryl (pink aquamarine) beads

4 2mm 18 karat gold daisy spacer beads

2 1½" 18 karat gold headpins with ball tip

1 pair of decorated 18 karat gold ear studs

PINK SAPPHIRE EARRINGS

(PICTURED ON OPPOSING PAGE, TOP LEFT)

YOU CAN OFTEN BUY DROPS, SUCH AS THESE SAPPHIRES, WITH WIRE LOOPS SO THAT THEY ARE READY TO USE AS LITTLE PENDANTS. UNLESS YOU ARE SKILLED AT WIRE-WRAPPING, BUYING THEM THIS WAY PRODUCES A BETTER FINISHED LOOK AND YOU CAN SKIP STEP 1.

1. If you are using beads without loops, start by making the wire loops for all the drops. Cut a piece of wire 1" long. Thread it through the hole of the bead and bend it back on itself so that about $3/16$" is above the bead, lying parallel to the tail of the wire.

2. Use the round-nosed pliers to make a loop on the tail so that the bottom of the loop touches the top of the other end of the wire. The wire should now look like a figure eight. Wrap the tail around the middle of the figure eight, enclosing the other end of the wire. Cut away any excess wire. Measure the excess wire and subtract that length from 1". Use this length to cut all the other pieces of wire so that they are exactly to size.

3. Open the jump rings and use them to attach the loops of the drops to each of the loops of the ear hoops.

TOOLS
Flat-Nosed Pliers, Round-Nosed Pliers, Wire Cutters

MATERIALS
14 6mm by 4mm faceted top-drilled teardrop pink sapphire beads with wire loops

14 2.5mm gold-filled jump rings

1 pair of gold-filled ear hoops with 7 loops

12" of 30 gauge gold-filled wire (if the beads did not come with loops)

BLACK SPINEL AND GARNET EARRINGS

(PICTURED ON PAGE 172, BOTTOM RIGHT)

HERE IS AN INTERESTING WAY TO USE CHAIN TO CREATE
EARRINGS. BY SELECTING THE CENTRAL LINK IN A THREE-
LINK PIECE OF CHAIN, IT ALLOWS ONE OF THE LINKS TO
FALL BACK ON TOP OF THE OTHER, MAKING A NICE FRAME
FOR THE TINY GARNET.

1. Start by using a jump ring to attach the middle link of a piece of
   chain to the loop of the earwire. When you hold up the earwire,
   one of the circular links should now fall down so that it is
   hanging over half the oblong link.

2. Add a garnet bead to a ½" headpin and attach it to the bottom of
   the pendulant circular ring by making a simple loop.

3. Add to a ¾" headpin a black spinel cone and a 2mm round gold
   bead. Make a simple loop and attach it to the bottom of the
   oblong link of the chain.

TOOLS
Round-Nosed Pliers, Flat-Nosed Pliers

MATERIALS

- 2 sections of chain, each with 2 circular
  links and 1 oblong link (The circular links
  are 10mm in diameter and the oblong is
  20mm in length.)
- 2 8mm faceted cone-shaped black spinel
  drops
- 2 1.5mm faceted round garnet beads
- 2 2mm hollow gold-filled round beads
- 2 ½" gold-filled headpins with ball tip
- 2 ¾" gold-filled headpins with ball tip
- 2 4mm gold-filled jump rings
- 1 pair of gold-filled earwires

CARNELIAN AND TURQUOISE EARRINGS (PICTURED ON PAGE 172, BOTTOM LEFT)

THE EASY WAY TO MAKE THESE EARRINGS IS TO BUY THE TURQUOISE CHAIN ALREADY PREPARED. BUT IF YOU ARE FEELING CONFIDENT IN YOUR ABILITY TO MAKE TINY WIRE-WRAPPED LOOPS AND HAVE TIME TO SPARE, YOU CAN MAKE THEM YOURSELF WITH LOOSE TURQUOISE BEADS AND 28 GAUGE GOLD-FILLED WIRE.

1. To each of the $1^1/_2$" eyepins, add a gold round bead, a vermeil disc, a carnelian bicone, a vermeil disc, and another gold round bead. Cut the eyepin about a $1/_4$" above the last bead and make a simple loop.

2. Attach the loop you have just made to one end of the turquoise chain. Use a 3mm jump ring to attach the other end of the chain to the earwire loop.

3. Use a 4mm jump ring to attach a vermeil flat disc to the loop of the eyepin.

TOOLS
Round-Nosed Pliers, Flat-Nosed Pliers, Wire Cutters

MATERIALS

2 10mm faceted carnelian bicone beads

2 34mm lengths ($1^3/_8$") of chain with 3mm turquoise round beads

2 11mm vermeil flat discs with stamped or cast design

4 3mm vermeil discs (torus)

4 2.5mm hollow gold-filled round beads

4 3mm gold-filled jump rings

2 4mm gold-filled jump rings

2 $1^1/_2$" vermeil eyepins

1 pair of vermeil earwires

TIP
You can make your own eyepins from 24 gauge gold-filled wire. Just cut the wire to the length you need, plus $1/_4$". Then make a simple loop at the end of the wire.

TANZANITE AND RUBY EARRINGS

(PICTURED ON PAGE 172, TOP RIGHT)

IT IS NOW QUITE COMMON TO FIND GEMSTONE DROPS SOLD WITH WIRE LOOPS ALREADY ATTACHED, MAKING THEM VERY EASY TO USE. AS LONG AS THE WIRE IS OF GOOD QUALITY, THIS IS A CONVENIENT WAY TO SAVE SOME TIME IN MAKING EARRINGS.

1. Start by creating the chain of tanzanite rondels. Cut the wire into 1" pieces. At the end of 1 piece of wire, make a very small wire-wrapped loop, only making 1 turn around (this should use about $^3/_8$" of the wire). Add a tanzanite rondel and make the beginnings of another wire-wrapped loop. Add a 3.5mm gold ring to the loop and finish it off with 1 turn around the base of the loop, making sure it is tight against the tanzanite bead.

2. At the end of another piece of wire, make the beginnings of a loop. Slip it over the ring that is attached to the link you have just made and finish it with 1 turn around. Add a tanzanite bead, start another loop, add another ring, and finish it off. Repeat this step another 4 times. You now have a chain of tanzanite beads with a ring at either end and 5 rings between the beads.

3. Add a tanzanite bead to a headpin and make the beginnings of a wire-wrapped loop. Add this to the first of the rings between the beads on the chain you have just made. Close the loop, wrapping the wire several times around the base. Add a tanzanite bead to another headpin and attach it to the same ring in the same manner. Repeat this process until there are 2 of these dangles on each of the rings between the tanzanite beads of the chain.

4. Use a 4mm jump ring to attach 3 of the ruby beads to the ring at one end of the chain.

5. Use a 3mm jump ring to attach the ring at the other end of the chain to the loop of the ear stud. Make the other earring in the same manner.

TOOLS
Round--Nosed Pliers, Flat--Nosed Pliers, Wire Cutters

MATERIALS

3	2mm by 3mm tanzanite faceted rondel beads
6	5mm by 7mm ruby faceted top—drilled drops (briolettes) with gold wire loops
	(If you cannot find the briolettes with wire loops, make wire-wrapped loops using 30 gauge gold-filled wire.)
14	3.5mm gold-filled rings
2	3mm gold-filled jump rings
2	4mm gold-filled jump rings
20	$^1/_2$" vermeil headpins with ball tip
12"	of 30 gauge gold-filled wire
1	pair of 18 karat gold ear studs

NOTE
You need very fine-tipped round-nosed pliers to make the wire-wrapped loops.

SEED PEARL EARRINGS

(PICTURED ON PAGE 177, CENTER)

THESE TINY PEARLS ARE CAPTURED IN A MINIATURE ABACUS
THAT DISPLAYS THEM OF AS A BROAD RECTANGULAR PATCH OF
COLOR AND LUSTER.

1. Place the two spacer bars side by side on a flat surface.

2. Put a charlotte on a headpin, and then thread the head pin through the first hole of one of the spacer bars.

3. Add five 3-millimeter pearls, and put the head pin through the first hole of the other spacer bar.

4. Add a charlotte, and make a simple loop the same size as that of the eyepin.

5. Repeat this for the second, fourth, and fifth holes of the spacer bars, leaving the center holes empty.

6. Cut the head off of the 11/2 inch headpin. Make a simple loop on the end the same size as the other loops you have made. Add a charlotte, and pass the pin through the center hole in the bottom of the second spacer bar (so all the loops are in the same direction).

7. Add five 3-millimeter pearls and pass the pin through the center hole of the top spacer bar.

8. Add a charlotte, the double daisy, a 4-millimeter pearl, a daisy, and a charlotte. Then finish off with a wire-wrapped loop and add the earwire.

9. Open the loops at the bottom, and add the silver balls.

TOOLS
Wire Cutters, Round-Nosed Pliers, Flat-Nosed Pliers (pliers must have very narrow tips)

MATERIALS

50	3mm side-drilled potato-shaped pearls in natural gray lilac or peacock color
2	4mm side-drilled potato-shaped pearls in natural gray lilac or peacock color
22	size 13/0 silver-plated charlottes
2	3mm sterling silver daisy spacer beads
10	2mm silver balls with loops
4	12mm five-hole sterling silver spacer bars
2	3.5mm sterling silver double daisy spacer beads
8	3/4" sterling silver headpins
2	1 1/2" sterling silver headpins
2	sterling silver earwires

BLUE-AND-GREEN PEARL EARRINGS (PICTURED ON PAGE 177, TOP)

TOP-DRILLED PEARLS CAN ALSO BE USED ON A VERTICAL AXIS TO CREATE AN INTERESTING OFFSET PATTERN.

1. To a headpin, add a silver bead, a blue pearl, three green pearls, and a silver bead. Make a simple loop to attach to the earwire.

TOOLS
Wire Cutters, Round-Nosed Pliers, Flat-Nosed Pliers

MATERIALS

2 dyed blue freshwater potato-shape pearls about 8—9mm in diameter

6 dyed green top-drilled teardrop pearls, approximately 6—5mm

4 2.5mm sterling silver round beads

2 1^1/$_2$" pieces of sterling silver long-and-short chain

2 1^1/$_2$" silver headpins with ball tip

2 sterling silver earwires

COIN PEARL EARRINGS

(PICTURED ON PAGE 177, BOTTOM)

YOU NEED VERY FINE-NOSED PLIERS TO CREATE THIS DESIGN—AS WELL AS GOOD EYESIGHT AND A DEGREE OF MANUAL DEXTERITY!

1. Cut the middle link of the chain making two 8-link pieces.

2. For dangles, add a charlotte to each headpin, a 3.5mm pearl, and another charlotte. Make a simple loop at the top.

3. Opening the loops, attach 7 dangles to each piece of chain by adding 3 to the bottom link and then 2 on each link above that.

4. Cut the wire into 2 equal pieces. Make a simple loop at one end and attach it to the top link of the chain. Add a coin pearl to the wire. Using the flat-nosed pliers to make a right angle, bend the wire about 1^1/$_2$" above the pearl. With the round-nosed pliers, bend the wire into a loop. Make 2 or 3 turns around the base of the loop and then bend the wire around the face of the pearl. There should be enough wire left over to make several final turns around the base of the bottom loop. For the second earring, wrap the wire in the opposite direction.

5. Add the earwires to the top loops.

TOOLS
Round-Nosed pliers, Flat-Nosed pliers

MATERIALS

2 7mm peach small coin pearls

14 3.5—4mm near-round pearls in peach, pink, or cream colors

28 size 13/0 gold-plated charlottes

1" gold-filled "Rolo" chain (about 19 links)

14" vermeil headpins with ball tip

3" 24-gauge gold-filled wire (half-hard)

2 gold-filled earwires

SILVER & GOLD BASICS

THE QUALITIES OF SILVER
AND GOLD

WHAT DO WE MEAN BY SILVER?

Although one of silver's greatest attributes is malleability, it is, in truth, just a little too soft to be ideal for making durable objects.

To increase its hardness, it is customary to add a little of another metal, usually copper. Because this practice is both ancient and widespread, a universal standard has developed: to be considered silver, an item must contain at least 92.5 percent silver. This is the definition of sterling silver, a term that was already in use in twelfth-century England. It is common to stamp larger silver objects with either the word silver or the number 925, which describes the fineness of the silver. Sterling silver has a fineness of 925 because it is 925 parts silver and 75 parts copper or other metal. In this book, when we say silver, we mean sterling.

THE COLOR OF GOLD

Fine or pure gold has a constant color, which is a slightly orange shade of yellow. When gold is alloyed with other metals, however, the color changes—sometimes dramatically. Some colors have come to be closely related to the karat value of the gold, while others have taken on a distinctive name like white, rose, or green gold. To preserve a color close to fine gold, producers use a balance of copper and silver. If they add more copper, the gold becomes redder; more silver, and it gets whiter. A little zinc or other metal is sometimes added to vary other characteristics of the alloy. White gold employs the bleaching qualities of palladium or nickel to achieve its silvery appearance, although it is often enhanced by a plating of rhodium. For most of us, the essential pleasing color of gold is yellow with just a touch of red.

KARATS AND CARATS

There are so many confusing measurements in the jewelry industry, but surely the most confusing expressions are karat and carat. The word (for they really are the same word despite the difference of an initial letter) is derived from the ancient Greek keration, or carob bean. As such, it was a unit of small weight, which became popular for measuring precious stones and metals. Because beans tend to vary in weight from place to place, there was a degree of variation and

OTHER TYPES OF SILVER

In northern Thailand, silversmiths use a softer silver to make it easier to form their intricate beads. The fineness of Thai silver can be anywhere from 950 to 985. Mexican jewelry also uses a 950 silver, which is softer than sterling. The expression fine silver refers to the highest grades of .999 and greater.

uncertainty for many centuries. In 1913, the United States settled on a metric carat, or 200 milligrams, as the measurement for the weight of gemstones, and this has since become the global standard.

KARAT GOLDS

Pure gold is also considered too soft for most jewelry: Gold alloys are a compromise of strength, hardness, color, and value. Throughout the world, 18 karat gold has a fineness of 750 and always contains 75 percent gold and 25 percent something else. The most popular karat golds are listed below with their percentages of pure gold and the corresponding fineness.

GOLD ALLOY STANDARDS

KARATS	% GOLD (FINENESS)	COMMENT
24	99% (990)	Popular in China and some other parts of the Far East
22	91.6% (916)	Popular standard in India
18	75% (750)	Most common global standard for gold jewelry
14	58.5% (585)	Popular standard in North America
12	50% (500)	Minimum to be described as gold in much of the world
10	41.7% (417)	Minimum to be described as gold in United States
9	37.5% (375)	Minimum to be described as gold in Canada and the U.K.

Many European countries insist that any items sold as gold are hallmarked or stamped by a government assayer's office to indicate their fineness. In North America, gold jewelry must be described by its karat quality, but independent assaying and physical marking is not required by law. Small items, such as individual beads, that would be ruined by stamping should be accompanied by an invoice or document marked with the karat quality and the name of the company that stands behind the mark.

Although to the layman a "heart of solid gold" seems straightforward, a jeweler would need to know whether that heart was 18 karat or mere 10 karat, for solid gold does not refer to its purity, only to the fact that the item is not hollow. The proportion of actual gold in a piece of jewelry is only determined by the karat mark or statement of fineness.

"PURE" GOLD

Although gold must be at least 99 percent pure to be 24 karat, there is also 24 karat fine gold which is 99.9 percent pure and used mainly for investment quality coins and bullion.

BUYING SILVER AND GOLD

Buying silver beads is fairly straightforward. If there is a reputable bead store near you, they should carry a selection of silver beads, either individually or on temporary strands. That selection should include seamless hollow rounds in several sizes, other spacer beads, and individual silver beads of character. All silver should be of sterling fineness (925) or higher. Silver beads are also widely available by mail order or online.

Gold beads can take a little more effort to acquire. A good bead store might carry a range of vermeil and gold-filled beads. When you are buying vermeil, you should select it for the color of the gold coating. Personally, I prefer vermeil to look like at least 18 karat gold. If you are going to buy a bead that is essentially colored silver, you may as well choose the color of gold you like best. When gold-platers describe vermeil as a specific karat, they are usually talking about the color they are trying to match rather than the precise gold content. Of course, the thickness of the plating is important, but unless you have access to an X-ray machine, you will not be able to tell. A decent plating should be expected to last a long time on beads that are not rubbed against other surfaces.

Buying real gold beads can require a little more searching and I list a few contacts in the resources section of the book. Gold bead and finding prices fluctuate with the price for gold as a commodity. In times when the gold price is rapidly changing, the price of gold jewelry components will follow the market. During periods when gold becomes more expensive, you can at least console yourself with the thought that any gold you already own has gone up in value. Your first question about any gold item should be regarding its purity or karat value. Despite their popularity in Asia, I find 24 and 22 karat golds too soft for jewelry. A respectable and very popular fineness in the United States is 14 karat, but since it is more than 40 percent some other metal, it can tarnish or react with sensitive skins. Personally, I prefer the more international standard of 18 karats—it is strong enough to maintain its appearance and, with 75 percent gold content, will not tarnish or affect the skin under normal wear. But this decision is simply a matter of taste and budget.

DEFINING GOLD-FILLED

To be called gold-filled (G.F.), an object must contain 10 karat (or better) gold, comprising at least one-twentieth of its gross weight. If the amount of gold used in this method is less than one-twentieth of the weight of the bead, then it is called rolled-gold. When buying gold-filled beads, 14 karat is a good fineness. The designation: 1/20 14K G.F indicates that at least one-twentieth of the weight of the item is 14 karat gold.

FAKING GOLD

The ancient alchemists never succeeded in their quest to turn base metals into gold, but several methods have been devised to make them look like gold.

GOLD PLATE

The most commonly used modern method is electrolytic plating, during which a very thin layer of gold is deposited on a base metal bead. To imagine how thin this layer is you must realize that it is measured by millionths of an inch and is hundreds of times thinner than a human hair. Beads and findings made by this process can

look attractive initially, but the normal wear of jewelry can rub away patches of the plating wherever it comes in contact with another object. I do not use gold-plated base metal in any of these projects because the objects possess little real value and are not suitable to use in fine jewelry.

GOLD-FILLED

Although gold-plated base metal is seldom an attractive material for fine jewelry, gold-filled often provides an inexpensive but respected alternative to real gold. In this method, the gold is fused or "sweated" on to the base metal by using heat and pressure. The bond is durable and because the layer is up to 200 times thicker than electroplating, the gold does not wear away under normal use.

VERMEIL

Fortunately, there is a much happier way to achieve the look and feel of gold jewelry at a modest cost. Although gold plating simply produces a gold-colored base metal, gold plating silver makes an admirable material called vermeil.

Nowadays, vermeil is produced through the same electrolytic method as gold plate. The official standard for designating an object vermeil is a layer of gold a hundred millionths of an inch thick over sterling silver. I suspect, however, that in the case of beads and findings, it is a thickness standard more honored in the breach than the observance. The great majority of vermeil beads are overlaid with a much thinner coating, although it is frequently of higher karat value than the minimum standard. In general, the term is used to indicate that the plating is real gold on real silver and you should expect that a bead referred to as vermeil is silver of at least sterling fineness and that it is coated in gold of at least 14 karats. Because the actual thickness of the plating can only be determined by an X-ray of the object, you should simply be aware that the plating, sooner or later, wears away.

For those who make their own jewelry, vermeil has another attraction: If the gold wears off, you can simply send the beads to an electro-plater and have them re-plated. So, except in the case of wire and some findings in which gold-filled is a better choice, use good-quality vermeil when you do not have the inclination or the budget to use solid gold.

STRETCHING IT OUT

There is a strong case for making a little gold or silver go a long way—both because they are expensive and because, well, you can! Good design ruthlessly exploits the metals' malleability to stretch them to the limit. Silver and gold are not just soft but have an extraordinary plastic quality that enables them to be beaten, pressed, and pulled into the thinnest of sheets or wires. With fine craftsmanship and creative thought these can be turned into an endless array of jewelry components.

FOIL (LEAF)

Gold and silver leaf or foil are at the extreme end of economy. With little effort, both metals can be pounded into leaves so thin and light that they will float like feathers on the air. A standard piece of silver or gold foil is as thin as one ten-thousandth of a millimeter, just a fraction of the thickness of a human hair.

This foil has been used for centuries to make base metal objects look like gold or silver. First a thin layer of varnish is applied to the metal. Then, using a fine brush and static electricity gathered by rubbing it on hair or fur, the leaf is picked up and laid onto the surface of the metal in a technique known as cold gilding.

But although foil is still sometimes used by jewelers to produce items like brooches or pendants, it is not practical for the surface of beads. The layer of gold or silver is simply so thin that it will be worn away as parts of a necklace rub against each other or against the skin. It is, however, a wonderful material for transforming glass beads into

FINDINGS KEY
Following Pages

1   2   3   4   5   6   7

8

9

10

11

12

13

14

15

16

17

18

19

20

21

22

23

24

25

26

27

28

29

30

31

32

33

34

35

36

37

38

39

40

41

exquisite little jewels. Lampwork or flame-worked glass beads are individually made by melting the tip of a glass rod over a flame or torch. The molten glass is gathered on a metal rod, then turned and molded into the required shape. Using different colored glass, the artisan can create beads of great complexity in a dazzling range of hues. Going one stage further, the highly skilled worker can also encase a piece of gold or silver foil between the layers of glass, adding a marvelous reflectivity and richness to the bead. Because the fragile leaf is encased in glass, it is protected from wear and, in the case of silver, from tarnishing. These glass foil creations are often among the most beautiful beads in the world and deserve a prominent place in the design lexicon of silver and gold jewelry.

SHEETS AND WIRES

Although leaf is too insubstantial to do anything except coat another material, thin sheets of gold and silver can be used to create beads and pendants. Cut into small pieces, they are shaped, bent, and fused to each other to build up larger objects that give an impression of

size and substance. Just as a house is constructed from thin ribs and sheets of wood, so beads can be created from these building blocks of silver and gold. Wires are used not only for connecting beads but to make the beads themselves. They are sometimes used independently to make light, basket-like beads but more often fused to the surface of sheets to create endless varieties of patterns.

HOLLOWNESS

Where gold and silver are concerned a hollow character can be a definite advantage. An ancient method of forming thin sheets of gold around a resin base is still used to create charming round beads that completely fool the eye and seem like solid gold until you pick them up and experience their extreme lightness.

Modern technology has also created a wide range of completely hollow gold and silver beads. The best of these are seamless and indistinguishable to the eye from solid metal. Indeed, it is almost pointless to buy plain round solid gold or silver beads when you can buy hollow beads for a small fraction of the price.

It is not just round beads that are hollow, however. Thousands of styles of silver and gold beads use the attribute of hollowness to reduce their weight and thus their cost. Many of the designs in these pages use hollow beads to make the jewelry affordable without losing any of its effect.

SWEET GOLD

For centuries it has been popular in India to decorate sweets and desserts with silver and gold. Hammered into gossamer-thin sheets called varak, the precious metals become so insubstantial that a mere breath would destroy them if they were not adhered to the surface of a sticky confection. Tasteless, odorless, and inert, they pass through the human body with no effect, their only purpose being to add a touch of glamorous extravagance to the dish.

WORTH YOUR WEIGHT IN GOLD

Gold is very, very heavy. Imagine a cube just fifteen inches high, fifteen inches deep, and fifteen inches wide. Sitting on your (strongly reinforced) dining table, it would occupy little more than the space required for a place setting. Yet, if it were made of solid 24 karat gold, it would weigh one ton, almost as much as a small car.

CARING FOR SILVER AND GOLD

SILVER

Admirable as it is in all other respects, silver has one small failing—it tarnishes. This is not common, everyday oxidation, like the rust on iron or the patina on copper, but a reaction with hydrogen sulfide that dulls its surface with a coating of silver sulfide.

Unfortunately, hydrogen sulfide is not uncommon in today's industrial air environments, and even lurks in the kitchen, emanating from innocent-looking onions and eggs. Keep silver away from items containing sulfur, particularly rubber, which will quickly form a nasty mark. Chlorine, bromine, and ozone also lead to silver tarnish, so both salty and polluted airs are quick to cause discoloring. Even if one avoids all of these, sterling silver has a small percentage of copper that oxidizes in ordinary clean air. After prolonged exposure to any air, most sterling silver begins to lose its bright gleam.

Often, the tarnish is just a slight patina that gives the silver a pleasant warmth, but if it becomes dull or black, it's time to recapture the sparkle. Fortunately simple polishing with a soft cloth removes light layers of tarnish, and heavier deposits can be quickly defeated using a commercial silver dip such as Goddard's. Be careful not to leave items in the dip longer than instructed. In general, thirty seconds in the dip, a rinse under fresh water, and a quick buff dry takes care of most jobs. Do not put gemstones into silver dip. When cleaning jewelry with a mixture of silver and gemstones, try to buff just the silver areas with a soft cloth or an anti-tarnish jewelry cloth.

Here's a clever way to clean silver using tin foil and a little baking soda, which relies on the fact that the metal aluminum is even more attracted to sulfur:

a) Line a pan with aluminum foil. Lay your silver items on the aluminum foil.

b) Boil enough water to cover the items in the pan. Add a dash of salt and a tablespoon or two of baking soda. (You can experiment with different proportions.)

c) While still very hot, pour this mixture over the silver and watch the tarnish slowly disappear. (The silver must be in contact with the aluminum foil for this to work.) When the tarnish is gone, rinse the items with fresh water and buff them dry with a soft cloth.

"GOOD" TARNISH

Remember that tarnish on some silver beads is to be appreciated rather than removed. Do not clean away all the black from antiqued beads, and think carefully before cleaning any silver beads that are genuine antiques—part of their appeal and much of their value might be in the patina you are about to destroy. Gold can be cleaned by rinsing it under warm water with a little liquid detergent, if necessary. To remove tarnish from low karat gold, use a little all-metal cleaner then rinse it under warm water before buffing dry.

I am told the method works because the aluminum takes the sulfur from the tarnish (silver sulfide) and leaves just the silver behind. The tarnish, in effect, turns back into silver. Some people like this method because they feel it does not actually remove any silver, which is the case in polishing or using a silver dip. But metallurgists point out that the bond holding this converted silver to the surface is fairly weak, and that it is probably lost when it is buffed dry.

However you clean the tarnish from your silver, you remove such a miniscule amount of the actual metal that solid silver objects will last for many generations. Silver plate should be treated much more carefully, as the thin layer of silver can be worn away by aggressive polishing.

To avoid tarnish, store your silver in a dry place wrapped in a soft cloth or acid-free tissue paper inside a zip-lock bag. If you expel the air from the bag and close it firmly, the silver should remain completely untarnished indefinitely. In practice, I usually forget about the cloth or paper and just put each individual piece in an airtight bag, which protects them from tarnishing and rubbing against other pieces of jewelry.

There are also patented formulas that protect against tarnish, like Tarni-Shield and a remarkable product originally developed at the British Museum called Renaissance Wax.

GOLD

Solid gold does not require any special protection when it is worn, except from scratching (and perhaps theft). It is wise, however, to remember that items made from vermeil or gold plate rely on the effect of a very thin layer of gold and should be kept away from situations in which the surface could be damaged by scratching or rubbing.

Some people are surprised when their gold shows signs of discoloration or tarnish. It is true that pure gold does not corrode, but the copper or silver that is mixed with lower karat gold is susceptible to chemicals in air, perspiration, and cosmetics. Thus, lower karat gold is far more likely to show signs of tarnishing than higher karat. More than 40 percent of 14 karat gold is some other metal, so it really isn't surprising that tarnishing occurs. If you find that low karat gold discolors on your skin, try wearing 18 karat or higher, which should solve the problem.

STORING GOLD JEWELRY

Whether gold or vermeil, it is best to keep necklaces in a soft jewelry roll with a layer of cloth between any other pieces of jewelry that might harm their surfaces. If you keep them in a box, avoid jumbling them up with other jewelry. The sharp surface of gemstones can scratch even solid gold.

PEARL BASICS

WHAT IS A PEARL?

It's ironic to think that a pearl begins life as something irritating! Irritating, that is, to some of the soft-bodied creatures called mollusks. It is even more unlikely that this exquisite gem is the work of a group of animals not famed for their glamour. The mollusks, after all, include slugs and snails as well as the rather more attractive shellfish. It's commonly believed that oysters produce pearls, but this is not, in fact, true. The commonly called "pearl oyster" is not of the Ostreidae family, and it usually only provides us with food for the eye. But let's not quibble over a name—"pearl oyster" sounds much more romantic than "pearl mollusk."

A KNACK FOR NACRE

Wherever they come from, whether they are natural or cultured, saltwater or freshwater, pearls have a common structure and share the same process of creation.

First, an irritant is introduced by accident or design into the mollusk. Presumably in an attempt to live more comfortably with the intruder, the animal then starts coating it with a hard, smooth substance called nacre (pronounced NAY-kur). More and more layers of nacre are deposited and, very slowly, a pearl starts to grow. In this way, the irritant becomes, we assume, more comfortable for the mollusk to live with and also transforms into something we treasure.

While many mollusks can perform this trick, what distinguishes valuable pearls from bits of dull, unwanted stone is the quality of the nacre covering. Some species just have a special knack for making a coat of iridescent magic. They don't do this exclusively to deal with annoying specks of grit, either. The entire inner lining of their shell is covered with this wonderful substance, giving us mother-of-pearl— another marvelous element for the jeweler's art.

THE SCIENCE BEHIND THE BEAUTY

Nacre itself is composed of two main substances: aragonite and conchiolin. Aragonite is a crystalline form of calcium carbonate, a very common mineral that makes up limestone, coral reefs, and shells. In a small way, shell-making mollusks are doing their bit for the environment since every molecule of calcium carbonate they make removes one of carbon dioxide from the atmosphere. Conchiolin, a more complex substance, is a glue-like protein that is excreted by the

SHAPE

The great majority of natural pearls are anything but round. That is why a strand of round, natural pearls of the same size and shape is so phenomenally expensive—it could take years to collect a set. Fortunately, all the different shapes of pearls can be just as attractive as rounds; sometimes, they are even more interesting.

THE OYSTER MYTH

Pearls are produced by a number of saltwater and freshwater shellfish. The famous sea-dwelling pearl makers are mostly of the genus sPinctada, although several other salt-water shellfish such as abalone and conch also create pearls. (Some would say that conchs do not make real pearls as they are not nacreous.) Indeed, the largest pearl in the world, a fourteen-pound, football-sized monster, was found in a giant clam. What comes as a surprise to many, however, is that a great number of pearls have always come from shellfish that live in rivers and lakes. No one even claims that these are oysters; we refer to them instead as pearl mussels. As modern pearl production focuses more and more on freshwater sources, the chances are ever greater that your pearls will have been produced by a humble mussel.

mollusk and binds together the aragonite crystals like bricks in a wall. Of course, this layering and coating process does not necessarily produce pearls that are round. But the unique way in which these translucent aragonite crystals are deposited gives the coating its ability to reflect and refract light. And it is this play of light that makes the pearl a gem. Because the nacre is translucent, light can reflect off the exterior surface as well as from layers just beneath the surface. This gives the pearl its particular warmth and depth—a unique luster unlike that of any other gemstone.

The different colors of pearls, which range from almost white to almost black, are often naturally occurring. Like most gemstones, however, the natural colors are sometimes enhanced through bleaching, heating, or even dyeing. If this is done within reasonable and customary limits, it is considered an agreeable way to treat a pearl. However, aggressive methods that could do long-term damage to the nacre, along with methods that make the enhancement imper-manent, are only acceptable in the cheapest pearls.

Whatever the variety—round or baroque, white or peacock blue, breathtakingly expensive or astonishingly cheap—the pearl is an ideal material for the jewelry designer's art. When displayed in the right setting, it has few rivals for attention.

THE VARIETIES OF PEARLS

NATURAL PEARLS

Today it is rare to find pearls for sale that have not been cultured. If you are lucky enough to have inherited a strand of natural pearls or acquired some in an estate sale, treat them with respect, but don't tuck them away in some hidden drawer. Pearls benefit from being worn. When you are confident enough in your design abilities, you might want to restring an old necklace to make a new, modern piece.

AKOYA PEARLS

Akoyas are round pearls cultured in the saltwater mollusk Pinctada fucata. Traditionally regarded as an exclusively Japanese product, large quantities of Akoya pearls are now produced in China. The nucleus of these pearls is a round bead made from the shell of an American mussel. As with all nucleated pearls, the layers of nacre can vary according to the length of time the pearl is left to grow. Gener-ally, the higher the number of nacre layers, the better the quality. Akoyas are seldom more than 9 millimeters in size.

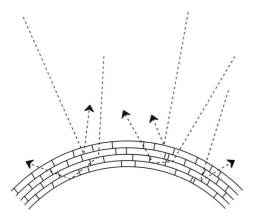

How pearls refelect light

NACRE COATING

The thickness of the nacre coating is extremely important to a pearl's value. Thick layers give the pearl more luster and greater longevity. Since freshwater, non-nucleated pearls are all nacre, the question of coating thickness does not arise. In nucleated pearls, however, producers have to compromise between the number of layers a mollusk will coat around the nucleus and the length of time they must leave it in the water to do its work.

SOUTH SEA PEARLS

These pearls are cultured in the South Pacific, particularly in Australia but also in Indonesia and the Philippines. They are nucleated in the same way as Akoyas and come in round or baroque (round but irregular) shapes. Grown in the Pinctada maxima mollusk, South Sea pearls are the largest of any commercially traded pearls, commonly measuring between 10 millimeters and 15 millimeters in size. It is not unheard of for South Sea pearls to reach more than 20 millimeters, but their cost increases dramatically in extremely large sizes.

TAHITIAN PEARLS

These large pearls are from the Pinctada margaritifera, or black-lipped oyster, the creature that produces the famous "black" pearls of the South Sea Islands. In reality, the colors of Tahitian pearls are not black but a subtle range of iridescent shades from a metallic gray to eggplant purple. Not all black pearls are Tahitian, however; instead, many are dyed pearls from other sources.

KESHI PEARLS

Keshis are serendipitous accidents of the culturing process. Occasion-ally, parts of the originally implanted mantle tissue break away and start forming separate irregular pearls of their own. There are also times when the nucleus bead is rejected altogether, leaving just the mantle implant to grow a freestyle pearl. Since the shapes have a wonderful variety and their all-nacre composition often gives them great luster and orient, keshi pearls have become much appreciated by jewelry designers.

FRESHWATER PEARLS

The culturing of freshwater pearls began in Lake Biwa in Japan in the 1930s. These "all-nacre" gems became so popular that the name "Biwa" has often been mistakenly used to denote any freshwater pearl. Due to pollution of the water, Lake Biwa produces very few pearls today. Luckily, the growing sophistication and quantity of Chinese freshwater pearls has brought prices back to levels that are attractive to a wide international market and has also led to a rapid increase in availability and variety.

While two decades ago the Chinese were producing tiny irregular pearls, scornfully dubbed "Rice Krispies" by the major players in the pearl market, they are now creating round, all-nacre pearls that rival Japanese Akoyas. Barring environmental disaster, it's likely that more and more of the pearls we wear will be coming from China.

FARM FRESH

Large-scale production of freshwater pearls has almost wholly shifted to the scattered patchwork of ponds that makes up China's pearl-farm industry.

No matter what the price or category of pearls you are buying, you should first establish that they meet the very basic standards:

* The holes must be drilled straight and centered.

* The nacre must be of a minimum thickness.

* The pearls must be even in appearance.

If the pearls you are considering do not meet these criteria, it is likely that the seller is just trying to clear a job lot of pearl rejects. Do not waste your valuable time on them. No matter how skillful your work, you will end up with something that looks cheap!

BUYING PEARLS

It is easy to buy pearls nowadays. Bead stores often carry a selection of freshwater pearls, either individually or on temporary strands. There are also mail-order and Internet sellers who have developed a reputation for quality and selection. There are even online auctions. Regardless of where you look, you should understand that the range of quality is very large. It is up to the customer to be discerning.

When you have established your budget, my advice is to go for luster first. It is better to compromise on size or shape or surface blemish than on the one value unique to pearls. Ask these questions:

* How deep is the warm glow from the pearl?

* Are the pearls' body color and overtones pleasing? Do they flatter the color of your skin and eyes?

* Is there any "orient," the iridescent rainbow-like play of light that will attract the attention and admiration your pearls deserve?

If you can answer these questions in the affirmative, or to your satisfaction, chances are you will be happy with your pearls for a very long time, whether they are big or small, round or Baroque.

It is best to examine pearls in good daylight. If the pearls are round or near round, put them on a flat white surface and roll the strand. You will quickly see how close to round they are. You can also detect any thinness in the nacre layers. Parts that are less lustrous than others will show up immediately because the duller patches will seem to "blink" at you. If the pearls are Baroque or another shape, turn the strand round between your hands and look for any unevenness of luster or serious blemishes.

In an inexpensive strand, a few flawed pearls are acceptable; put them at the very back of a necklace or just don't use them. If the pearls seem too perfect and you are worried that they may not be real, you can look at them through a jeweler's loupe (a 10x magnifying glass). Real pearls should show at least some irregularities when magnified.

PEARL STRAND KEY

(PAGES 196–197, FROM LEFT TO RIGHT)

1. Tahitian Black Baroque
2. Akoya Near Round
3. Silver-Rice
4. Pink Potato
5. Drops
6. Seed
7. Top-Drilled Button
8. Top-Drilled Drop
9. Side-Drilled Potato
10. Lilac Near Round
11. Akoya Round
12. Facetted Round
13. Mixed Peach, Pink, Lilac, White Top-Drilled Peanut
14. Keshi
15. Stick
16. Coin

1 2 3 4 5 6 7 8 9

10 11 12 13 14 15 16

CARING FOR PEARLS

Since it is partly composed of organic material, nacre tends to deteriorate over time. Whether the attractive qualities of a pearl last for centuries or for just for years depends both on the thickness of the nacre and on the care with which the pearls are treated. Most pearl sellers coyly suggest that their pearls will last "a lifetime," "for generations," or "for "decades"—as long as they are "properly cared for."

Pearls certainly require more care than other gems. Although you don't have to actively work at keeping them alive, it is good to know what dangers to avoid.

The old adage "a woman should put her pearls on last" is a good one. The wisdom behind this advice is meant to spare the pearls from being coated with perfume, hair spray, or any other cosmetic materials that might hasten their demise. Acid is death to pearls! Cleopatra was said to have dissolved a priceless pearl in wine and drunk it in order to show Mark Anthony that, where extravagance was concerned, she had no equal. (Instead, it ended up being an object lesson in how not to treat a pearl—or an empire.)

Although pearls should be kept away from anything acidic, a little moisture is good for their health. Pearls naturally contain a tiny percentage of water, and they are best preserved in an environment that does not change their composition. Excessive dryness can cause pearls to crack, so store them in a case or pouch lined with soft material somewhere with at least a little humidity. If your skin is acidic, it is a good idea to wipe your pearls with a damp cloth after wearing. A little olive oil can also be good for pearls if you feel like pampering them.

In general, however, you should simply keep your pearls away from acidic or corrosive substances. Do not store them in an excessively dry place or in a box with a bunch of other jewelry that might damage their surface. Of course, try not to drop them on hard surfaces or scratch them. And remember, cats and children have no business playing with your pearls!

GLASS BASICS

TYPES OF GLASS USED FOR BEADS

SODA-LIME GLASS

This is the simplest and most common of glasses, forming most of our windows and light bulbs. It is composed primarily of silicon dioxide (from quartz sand), sodium oxide, and calcium oxide—a combination that has served glassmakers for several thousand years and is still widely used today.

BOROSILICATE GLASS

Very sudden changes in temperature can cause ordinary glass to shatter, an unfortunate event if it happens to hold the contents of your family's dinner or the results of a scientist's chemistry experiment. The challenge of making heat-resistant glass was overcome in Germany at the end of the nineteenth century by adding the mineral boron.

As a result, chemistry labs are able to use test tubes and retorts without fear of destruction, and the glass pie dish has become one of the most common pieces of household cooking equipment. Although borosilicate glass needs a hotter flame to work, it also has some qualities that are attractive to lampwork beadmakers—it is crystal clear, difficult to break, and relatively easy to work with.

LEAD CRYSTAL

The art of making glass that was "crystal clear" long eluded large-scale producers. Then, in the thirteenth century, the Venetians combined pure quartz sand with ash from sea plants to create a glass of such clarity that they called it cristallo, after the clear rock crystal that it emulated. Others tried to imitate the Venetian product, but it was only surpassed in the seventeenth century when an Englishman named John Ravenscroft devised (with a little Venetian help) a commercial process to make a glass that was not only brilliantly clear but also easily cut to produce sharp, reflective surfaces. Part of the secret was the addition of a large amount of lead oxide, typically more than one quarter of the total compound. Today, lead crystal sets the standard for the highest quality crystal glass and is used to dazzling effect in beads.

DICHROIC GLASS

This is truly a high-tech glass that came out of space industry research and is dependent on the same physics that cause the rainbow effect in soap bubbles. Dichroic glass is made by vaporizing metallic salts in a vacuum so that they coat the surface of the glass. This produces a glass with a stunning iridescence, similar to that of the "fire" found in opals. Dichroic glass is expensive and difficult to work with, but when fused to certain kinds of other glass, it can be used to great effect in lampwork beads. Because the firing of dichroic glass changes its characteristics, each bead is original and unique.

LEAD GLASS

The addition of lead oxide to glass makes it softer, easier to work with at lower temperatures, and easier to cut and re-melt. Some lampwork and pressed beads use glass with a small amount of lead oxide.

GLASS BEAD VARIETIES

With few exceptions, the style, complexity, and cost of a glass bead is dependent on the method used to make it rather than on the glass itself. So important is this factor in the selection of glass beads that we use the production process as the first label in categorizing them. To know anything about glass beads, therefore, you have to know something about how they are made. The following is a description of the main types of glass bead production.

LAMPWORK

One of the earliest methods of bead-making was to melt a bit of glass and then wind it around a metal rod. Once the glass had cooled and hardened, you would take out the rod and be left with a round object with a hole in its middle—a bead. For obvious reasons, beads made in this way are referred to as wound glass. A more sophisticated version of wound glass was developed when beadmakers realized that if they kept the glass on the rod hot enough, they could add different colors of glass on top; all they needed was a flame directed toward the developing bead. At first the flame was supplied by an oil- or tallow-burning lamp, which gave the name lampwork to the beads produced in this way (they are also referred to as flamework). Since the flame of a lamp was not hot enough to melt the glass, beadmakers would blow air through a thin pipe and into the flame, increasing its heat and directing it toward the bead. A bellows was soon added to save the beadmakers' lungs although the ancient method of mouth blowing is still used in India.

Modern technology has replaced the old lamps with high-intensity torches that combine fuel and oxygen to focus high heat with pinpoint precision. Regardless of whether the heat source is a lamp or a torch, this type of bead-making provides the greatest scope of imagination, skill, and creativity both to the artist and to the artisan.

Since each bead is produced by hand, each is, to a degree, unique. The beadmaker starts with a selection of thin glass rods in different colors. Taking a long metal needle about the diameter of the hole of the bead, she or he melts the tip of a glass rod over a hot torch (the "lamp" or "flame") and catches the molten glass on the metal needle. As she or he twists the needle, the beadmaker can gather the molten glass in a ring around the needle. By keeping this core red-hot and melting other rods, she or he can add different colors and press or stretch the bead into whatever shape the design, or his or her imagination, calls for.

GLASS BEAD KEY

Page 202
1. Lampwork Opaque Glass
2. Various Lampwork Designs
3. Lampwork with Gold Foil
4. Charlottes
5. Pressed Glass with Seed Beads
6. Pressed and Coated Glass
7. Lampwork Dichroic Glass
8. Pressed Glass

Page 203
1. Chevron Beads (Venice)
2. American Lampwork (Nancy Pilgrim)
3. Millefiore (Venice)
4. Dichroic Glass (Luigi Catelan)
5. Bugle Beads
6. Bohemian Lampwork
7. Furnace Glass (Art Glass)
8. American Dichroic (Nikki Blanchard)
9. Glass Crystal
10. Seed Beads
11. Lampwork with Silver Foil (Bohemian)
12. Millefiore (Venice)
13. Pressed Glass
14. Blown Glass
15. Lampwork with Gold Foil

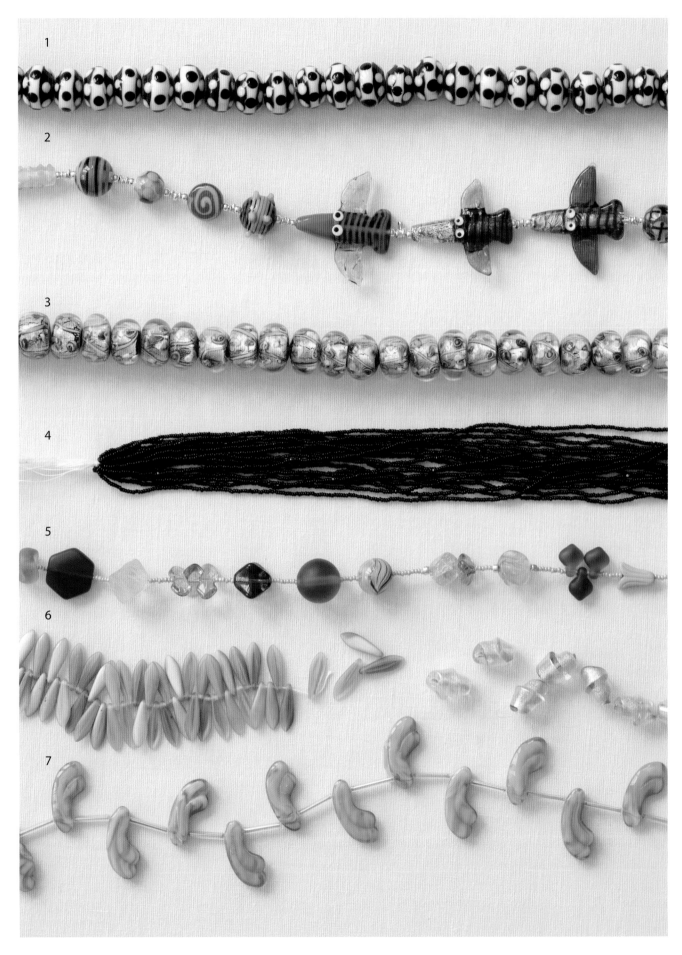

1

2

3

4

5

6

7

1

2

3

4

5

6

7

8

9

10

11

12

13

14

15

Because lampwork beads are the most labor-intensive to produce, they are generally the most expensive type of glass bead.

The production of lampwork beads is still a cottage industry in some parts of the world, with companies delivering glass rods to the homes of beadmakers and collecting their finished beads. The Czech Republic, Italy, Japan, India, and China all have important lampwork industries, but the most surprising development has been the renaissance of glass bead-making in the United States. Starting with just a handful of enthusiasts in the 1970s, American beadmakers now number in the thousands and include some of the most highly respected lampwork bead designers in the world.

DRAWN GLASS

Molten glass is amazingly elastic and can be stretched to great lengths without breaking. If you heat a blob of molten glass in a furnace, attach it to one end of a hollow metal tube, and give a good blow in the other end, the glass will expand like a balloon. Beadmakers have long used this quality to create the holes in beads. Simply puff to create a pocket of air, attach another rod to the other end of the red-hot balloon of glass, and start stretching. As the glass stretches out into a cylinder, the bubble of air is also stretched out, becoming smaller and smaller as the cylinder turns into a tube. Once the glass tube cools, it can be cut into small pieces; the trapped pocket becomes the hole of a bead. Since drawn glass can be stretched very evenly, all the little pieces cut from the tube look pretty much the same. And since it can be stretched very far—two to three hundred feet is not unusual—this method enables glass-workers to make hundreds or thousands of beads out of one batch of glass, a much easier process than to create them one by one over a hot flame.

Among the most commonly used products of this method of bead-making are seed beads. This is a generic term applied to very small glass beads produced in large quantities.

Any glass beads that are under four or five millimeters in diameter and do not have some obvious distinction (like the faceting of crystals) risk being lumped into this category. In modern processes the hot glass tube is not drawn by hand, but by gravity fed onto a conveyer or pulled by a wheel that draws it out at a constant speed. As the glass tube cools, it is cut into shorter lengths that are then chopped by a machine into tiny beads. These are then heated, tumbled, and polished to form rounded, smooth edges. The finished seed beads are either strung into hanks or sold by weight. Bugle beads are made the same way, except they are cut into longer lengths and their ends are not polished; so, you can see what a cane looks like before it is broken up into seed beads.

Glass canes are another product of the drawn glass method. Because molten glass stretches so evenly, any pattern or design it starts out with remains intact through-out the entire piece, simply getting smaller and smaller as the cane gets longer. By bundling together several layers or rods, beadmakers can easily create a design in a short, fat piece of glass and then stretch it out into a long, thin rod. When they cut the rod into little pieces, the end pattern of each piece will be exactly the same—a seemingly impossible, perfect miniature of the original. Venetian artisans were particularly famous for this kind of intricate glass work, even incorporating portraits of well-known people into their designs.

A contemporary example of the drawn glass method is a type of bead called furnace glass or art glass. While many glass beads start in a furnace, where the glass is melted, this expression has come to refer to a particular kind of modern drawn glass bead, one in which the core of the rod is coated with a clear glass. This kind of bead requires a large annealing kiln so that the bead can cool very slowly in order to avoid cracking.

BLOWN GLASS

Just as vases and bottles can be made by blowing air into a blob or, more elegantly expressed, a "gather" of molten glass, so, too, can beads be created by blowing glass on a small pipe to create a bubble-like shape. It is easier, however, to start with a thin-walled glass tube into which air can be blown by mouth or bellows. While individual and free-form beads can be made this way, larger-scale production is achieved through the use of heated glass tubes contained within a mold. One end of the tube is sealed. As air is blown into the other end, the sides of the tube expand to fill the bead-shaped areas of the mold. When the glass cools, there is a chain of glass bubbles that can be cut apart to make individual beads. This kind of bead was once popularly used to imitate pearls. After the bead chain was formed, a solution made of fish scales (called essence d'orient) was blown to coat the interior surface with a nacre-like sheen. The beads, filled with wax to make them appear solid, had a remarkably fine pearl-like appearance that could not wear off, as it was

on the inside of the glass.For the jewelry designer, one of the attractions of blown glass beads is that they can be both very large and very light. While they seem as if they should be too fragile for constant wear, they are surprisingly sturdy.

PRESSED GLASS

Pressed glass beads are produced in great number through a semi-mechanical process. First, a metal mold is created. The mold is in two halves. Each half has the shapes of a dozen or more beads side-by-side. The beadmaker uses thick glass rods, each about an inch in diameter. The beadmaker sits in front of a pressing machine with the glass rods sticking in a small furnace by his side. Once the end of a glass rod is the right temperature, the beadmaker lays it on the bottom half of the mold; the top half is then pressed down, forming the shape of the beads. At the same time, a set of metal needles is thrust into holes in the side of the mold, piercing the glass to form the holes of the beads. The strip of beads comes out of the mold attached by a thin edge of glass. The beads are then broken off the

strip, placed into a tumbling machine with sand or some other abrasive material, and tumbled for several hours to remove the edges and polish the glass to an even, smooth surface. With fire-polished beads, the rough pressed-glass beads are "polished" by being placed into a hot oven; the surface of the glass begins to melt and develops an attractive shine unique to this method.

COATED GLASS

Glass beads are often given distinction by the use of various surface coatings, on either the outside of the bead or the interior of the hole. The inventiveness of beadmakers has resulted in the creation of numerous methods, including glazing, etching, gilding, metalizing, staining, painting, iridizing, platinizing, and lustering—all of which can either subtly or completely change the characteristics of the original bead.

A popular coating is Aurora Borealis, or AB for short. As its name suggests, this coating adds a multihued iridescence to the surface.

Glass beads can also be metalized, or covered in metals, such as silver and gold. A particular style of seed bead called silver-lined gets its inner sparkle from having the hole lined with a metallic solution, giving it a silvery sheen.

CUT CRYSTAL

Like gemstones, glass can be faceted by cutting or grinding. Although this method is much more expensive than creating faceted pressed-glass beads, the difference is enormous. Even the best pressed and fire-polished glass beads lack the sharp edges and finely planed surface of cut glass. Because of its exceptional clarity and reflectivity, only crystal glass is used in this method. The best of these cut crystal beads, such as Swarovski, display a sparkle and brilliance that is a serious rival to the gemstones they often emulate. Cut crystal beads are prized for their precision and glitter and can be used to produce stunning jewelry. Sophisticated modern techniques are used to make them; consequently, their production methods are often cloaked in secrecy. More than a hundred years ago, the Swarovski family moved its production from the glass bead capital of Gablonz to the small village of Wattens, high in the Austrian Alps. There they found not only a source of hydro-electric power to operate their cutting machines but also a remote situation in which the confidentiality of their methods could be closely guarded.

PATÉ DE VERRE AND POWDERED GLASS

When glass is crushed and powdered, it can be mixed into a paste that can then be applied to a mold and fired to become fused and solid. While this method sounds very simple and can, if used casually, produce clumsy-looking beads, it can also, in the right hands, create beads of great intricacy and beauty. But it is a labor-intensive process and mainly practiced by individual artisans.

In Africa, colorful glass beads are made by crushing old glass into a powder and then mixing it into a paste with gum Arabic, which is then shaped and heated. The base core is then coated with more colored glass paste and heated again to form a patterned surface. Older beads made in this manner are often highly valued by collectors.

GEMSTONE BASICS

ABOUT GEMSTONES

If you have only a hazy understanding of what makes a "stone" into a "gemstone," you have plenty of company. There are, quite literally, hundreds of types of gemstones, and new ones are being "discovered" and "created" every year as the potential of previously scorned minerals and new technologies is recognized and exploited. Although the market knows a gemstone when it sees it, dictionaries and reference books offer paltry guidance in their definitions. Descriptions include: "a rock that can be cut and polished to be used for jewelry," "an attractive and valuable piece of mineral," "a stone that exhibits qualities of brilliance, luster, fire, etc.," and "a mineral with a crystalline structure." One authoritative guide even goes so far as to say, "There is no generally accepted definition for the term gem or gemstone." That gemstones are "minerals" and "rocks" is mostly undisputed, although these terms can also be imprecise. A mineral is inorganic, something neither "animal" or "vegetable" in nature; yet, both jet and diamonds start off as organic matter, amber is the fossilized resin of trees, and pearls are made by mollusks. Rock and stone are usually aggregates of minerals, but in the case of gem "stone" they can also be one single mineral or even a single element. Rocks are forms of chemical compounds created, with a few exceptions, by a geological process. They are forged in the earth by heat, pressure, and chemical reactions. They have a defined and compact molecular structure, often crystalline, which makes them hard. Along with hardness, they have other physical characteristics that make them relatively easy to identify.

But when is a mere mineral or rock a "gem" stone? When it is rare, perhaps, and found only in a few locations, such as larimar? But quartz is one of the most common minerals on earth and it is a gemstone! When it is crystal clear, such as, well ... crystal? But black onyx is utterly opaque and it is a gemstone! When it is very expensive perhaps, such as emerald? A fine strand of green emeralds could buy a container load of green aventurine, but the latter is also a gemstone. When it is more valuable than any other jewelry components? Yet some ordinary gemstone beads are cheaper than some glass beads! And even good-quality faceted beads can be less expensive than the best glass-crystal faceted beads.

So what, exactly, does define a gemstone? About the only things that all gemstones have in common is that they are hard enough to be polished (although some are not) and attractive enough that people want to use them in jewelry. Whether it is a "gem" or merely a rock is in the eye of the beholder and the judgment of the marketplace.

PRECIOUS OR SEMIPRECIOUS

Because the definition of a gemstone is so subjective and broad, there has traditionally been an effort to separate the "men from the boys," or "precious" from "semiprecious." The definition used to be quite simple—diamonds, rubies, sapphires, and emeralds were "precious" and all the others were in some way inferior, or "semiprecious." But, in today's gemstone market, a fine piece of imperial topaz has far more value than a similar piece of ordinary sapphire. Paraiba tourmaline is far more rare and expensive than most diamonds. Alexandrite is more valuable than most rubies.

One might think that these disparities could be rectified by adding more gemstones to the "precious" category, but the issue is further complicated by the fact that quality is everything. Some gemstones, such as rose quartz, can be found both at the very lowest end of the "semi" leagues, as well as mixing with the players in the "precious" teams, depending entirely on the quality of the individual piece. Equally, there are some sapphires and rubies that just don't make it in the quality stakes and are relegated to being extremely "affordable," if not downright "cheap."

Because the terms "precious" and "semiprecious" add more confusion than clarity, I don't use them, but I do try to define some of the properties of gemstones that create quality and value. The difference in cost and desirability between a 4mm hematite "gemstone" and a 5 carat diamond "gemstone" is immense, and this chapter explains why.

THE NATURE OF GEMSTONES

The physical nature of gemstones is a subject that appeals more to rock collectors, scientists, and gem merchants than it does to jewelry makers, who are generally more interested in aesthetics than physics. Should you want to know that the chemical description of aquamarine is $Al_2Be_3Si_6O_{18}$, that topaz has perfect cleavage, or that the refractive index of iolite is about 1.54, there are many books available that list the exact chemical composition, crystal system, hardness, cleavage, refractivity, and other defining physical characteristics of gems. It is, however, interesting to have an understanding of the methods by which gemstones are identified, and it is sometimes useful to appear knowledgeable in the eyes of gemstone sellers, if only to have them understand that you are not someone who can be deceived by serpentine dressed up as jade or howlite pretending to be turquoise.

CRYSTAL STRUCTURE

Most, but not all, gems are crystalline forms of minerals. Just like crystals of common salt, their molecules are arranged geometrically in such a way that a series of flat surfaces is created. These crystals can be created in various ways—from the furnaces of molten magma or lava, under the immense pressure of the earth's crust, or even from watery solutions. Whatever their origins, all crystals have certain defined characteristics and fall within one of seven families or "systems," a feature that helps gemologists to identify them and cutters to avoid destroying them. All crystals, even diamonds, can break, and many tend to break along predictable lines. If a gem breaks cleanly along a certain plane, it is said to have good "cleavage." Many crystals have no cleavage at all, but all have distinct ways they "fracture," or break unevenly. Aside from making you sound clever if you can drop the terms "cleavage" or "fracture" into a conversation about gems, these terms are of no practical use to you and can be immediately forgotten. "Hardness" is a different matter.

HARDNESS

This quality of gemstones is so important that a simple scale was created to rank them from 1 to 10 in order of increasing hardness. On the Mohs scale, named after its Austrian inventor, the softest mineral, talc, can be scratched by a fingernail, whereas the hardest, diamond, can be scratched by nothing else except another diamond. For the proper care of jewelry and to understand what gems are appropriate companions when creating a design, it is important to know a little about their relative hardness. For example, once you are aware that fluorite (Mohs 4) can be scratched by a knife, you will be sure not to store it with the cutlery nor set it on a strand between faceted beads of quartz, which, at 7 on the scale, is hard enough to scratch glass, which is a middling 5. Hardness is one of the reasons that diamond is the sole occupant of the royal throne of gemstones. Although rubies and sapphires clock in at an impressive 9 on the scale, they are 140 times less hard than diamonds, which rank at number 10. In general, I tend to think of any gemstone that can be scratched by glass, that is to say, less than a 5 on the Mohs scale of hardness, as being soft and requiring special care. Because anything less than 7 can be scratched by quartz, a component of common dust, gems in the 5 to 7 range category are hard but should be stored carefully. Stones of 8 or greater can generally look after themselves, but nothing should be allowed to rub against diamonds, which will damage the surface of any other gem. Hardness is, of course, one of the ways in which genuine stones can be distinguished from glass imitations because a gem scratches, yet is not scratched by, a material lower on the scale.

Density, or the weight of an object relative to its volume, is another useful way for gemstone dealers to distinguish one stone from another, and the range of specific densities of all gems is carefully charted. Measuring density, however, is not convenient for most buyers because it requires a hydrostatic scale or a series of heavy liquids, most of which are toxic. But, once you become familiar with buying gemstones, the weight of a strand can often tell you something about its nature. A strand of cubic zirconia (CZ), one of the densest of gems, is quite easily distinguished from a strand of similar glass crystal because the CZ feels much heavier in the hand.

COLOR

It is the properties of gemstones that are visible to the eye that are of overriding interest to the jewelry designer and to the wearer. Of these, color is often the primary consideration and seems to be a straightforward, inherent quality of the stone. Yet color is also a slippery character when it comes to identifying and categorizing gems. A single type of gemstone can exhibit a variety of colors or a range of tones, many of which are achieved through heat treatments or other enhancement processes. Indeed, classifying stones by color can cause confusion to both professionals and amateurs: sapphire comes from the Greek for "blue," and so it always used to be, but today sapphires come in many different colors—except red, when they are called rubies. Hematite comes from the Greek for "blood red," but it is dark gray. Diamond dealers refer to other gems as mere "colored" stones, but diamonds have always been found in shades of blue, black, and yellow, as well as the more typical "colorless." Turquoise is always blue, except when it's green; garnets are always red, unless they are "grossular," "spessartite," or "andradite." Aquamarine was once prized for its "sea green" color, but nowadays many people prefer its "sky blue" variety. The color "topaz" is a yellow-hued golden brown, but the gemstone also comes in blue, pink, and green. Kunzite and alexandrite change color depending on the angle from which you observe them, a quality called pleochroism. The word "amethyst" immediately makes you think "purple," but nowadays there is a fashion for turning it green. Indeed, the moment you insist a gem is always a certain color, it is begging someone to show you that it's not. But if color is confusing to those who classify gems, it is a simple matter to those who use them—it is either pleasing or it is not. As a jewelry maker, your eye tells you most of what you need to know!

REFLECTION AND REFRACTION

The other essential quality of a gem is how it reflects light. All gemstones, particularly the opaque ones, depend on luster, or the way light reflects from their surface, for part of their effect. Luster ranges all the way from "splendent," reflecting all the light like a mirror, to "dull," reflecting hardly any light. In between is a range of effects described as "adamantine" (like diamond), "vitreous" (like glass), "metallic," "waxy," "pearly," "greasy," "resinous," and "silky." The majority of gemstones used for jewelry have a vitreous luster. Most transparent and many translucent gems also produce reflections from their internal surfaces. In the case of faceted transparent stones, the lower facets act like a mirror to reflect the light back up through the face of the stone. This is particularly important for colorless stones that are often cut to reflect the maximum possible amount of light from the lower facets, an effect known as "brilliance." Most gemstones also refract, or bend, light as it passes through them. This is useful to those who need to precisely identify gemstones—light bends differently in different types of gemstones and each finds its own position in an index of refraction. Some colorless gemstones also disperse light, breaking it into the colors of the rainbow, a quality that accounts for the "fire" in diamonds. Others achieve magical color effects through interference, where the light is broken into many different colors by the internal structure of the stone. These pleasant accidents of light—sometimes sparkling, sometimes subtle—include "iridescence," "opalescence," and "play-of-color." Precious opals and labradorite use this trick spectacularly, whereas pearls and moonstone content themselves with a more modest shimmering of hues. Occasionally, the internal structure of the stone reflects the light in a particular pattern, like the star effect of some rubies and sapphires, or the "chatoyancy" of all tiger's-eye.

INCLUSIONS AND OTHER "FLAWS"

Like all natural materials, gemstones exhibit natural variations, and it is seldom that any of them are completely "clean" of foreign matter, cracks, or irregularities in their structure. Although these used to be seen as "flaws," modern gem dealers understand that they can often be an asset. There is little doubt that a fifty-million-year-old insect encased in a piece of amber is an addition that makes the stone far more valuable than it would be without it. Some types of gemstone, such as rutilated quartz, even depend on their inclusions to provide value, whereas others such as lazurite look much better with specks of another mineral thrown in. Because the beauty of any gem is a matter of opinion, you should seek your own advice when deciding whether an inclusion is a mark of character or an unfortunate scar. Even cracks and cavities can sometimes lend an attractive character to a gem, but they are more often real flaws, marring the reflective qualities of the surface and weakening the integrity of the stone. Comparison with other qualities of the same gemstone helps you determine whether they add interest or cheapen the stone.

ENHANCEMENTS

In today's market, the entirely natural gemstone, untouched by any cosmetic treatment, is probably in the minority. The methods of enhancement have become so good and so difficult to detect that it is better for the buyer to assume a stone has been enhanced until proven natural. You can be certain that anything that can be done to make a gemstone more attractive will be done, whether it is oiling, waxing, heat-treating, irradiating, dyeing, acid-treating, coating, impregnating, reconstituting, or some technique that has only recently been invented and is still a mystery to the market.

Enhancement is not, in itself, a bad thing. The industry has come to accept that these treatments often improve gemstones and certainly deliver to the desiring public a far greater selection and quantity than would be possible without them. Indeed, some gemstones would not exist without enhancement: topaz is rarely found in a natural blue color; yet, wonderful shades, such as London blue, sky blue, and Swiss blue, have in the past few years begun adorning the necks of women around the world. The secret is the sophisticated heat treatment and irradiation of colorless topaz stones. Enhancement is positive unless it steps over the line of fair practice. That line is quite nicely drawn in the U.S. Federal Trade Commission guidelines that require a gemstone seller to disclose enhancements if it "has been treated in any manner that is not permanent or that creates special care requirements." Because most enhancements achieve permanent change, it is only those that fail or that are knowingly temporary that should concern the buyer. Unfortunately, there are plenty of those, and many cannot be detected until too late. Several years ago, a large quantity of chalcedony in India was subjected to a botched acid treatment, producing beautiful colors that were snapped up by dealers and customers around the world. It was only some months later that the colors began to fade and acid that had not been permanently combined with the stone began corroding the beading wires and findings. Ever since, I have bought and sold nothing but natural chalcedony, even though the coloring techniques are probably perfected by now. Few failed enhancements are quite as dramatic as that, however. Instead, over time surfaces become duller, colors paler. Of course, this also happens with some natural gemstones if they are not properly cared for. In the case of cheaper stones the fading of their charms might not be too bothersome, but it is certainly a major concern with more expensive gems and should be taken into consideration when purchasing.

SYNTHETICS

Synthetics are gemstones that are made in the laboratory or workshop. Often identical in composition to the natural stone, they are accepted additions to the supply of gems. Although there is hardly any stone that cannot be created synthetically, the high cost of production makes it economical for only the higher value gems to be created in the expensive furnaces of the laboratory. Another, less expensive type of synthesis is called reconstruction, and it is practical for some cheaper gemstones. In this process, the material is splintered or powdered and then heated and pressed to form larger pieces. Almost all hematite beads are made this way and turquoise, amber, lapis lazuli, and coral are sometimes given this treatment.

IMITATIONS

Because most gemstones have a vitreous, or glassy, luster and transparency, they are often imitated by glass, and it is sometimes difficult to tell the difference. Real gemstone frequently shows natural irregularity and inclusions that glass cannot match without time-consuming techniques, and there is often a perceived "life" in natural stone that glass can never quite imitate. Gemstones are also imitated by other gemstones, both natural and synthetic. Diamond is constantly being chased by other colorless stones that come close to mimicking its optical qualities, although its hardness has never been equaled. There is nothing wrong with any of these imitations as long as they are clearly described as such and not foisted off as the "real thing."

FAKES

Materials that masquerade as gems have been a problem in the marketplace as long as jewels have existed. Today, there is a good arsenal of techniques to distinguish fakes, but many of them require an inconvenient and expensive trip to the gemological laboratory. Small and inexpensive heat-resistance testers are beginning to become available, and these can be a good investment if you are producing a lot of gemstone jewelry. For the most part, however, you need to rely on the reputation of the seller to help you avoid an unfortunate purchase.

GEMSTONE BEAD CUTS

SMOOTH ROUNDS AND RONDELS

Almost all opaque gemstones and most of the colored transparent ones are available as smooth round or rondel beads. Some gems, such as iolite, peridot, garnet, and kyanite, are rarely seen in sizes greater than 4mm or 6mm. Most colorless stones are faceted to display their reflective properties better, although rock crystal and moonstone are also made into smooth rounds.

OTHER SMOOTH SHAPES

Many stones are cut as cabochons, circular or oval shapes with a domed front and a flat back, and set in gold or silver to form pendants. There are many other shapes of smooth gemstones that are drilled as beads. These range all the way from large ovals and lozenges, to small stars, crosses, and discs. The variety of shapes increases every year as inventive cutters explore the possibilities of different gemstones.

NUGGETS AND SHARDS

Sometimes, rough pieces of gemstone are tumbled to form polished nuggets or pebbles. If the crystalline structure of the stone is suitable, they can even be left unpolished in shards and whole crystals. These "rough" shapes can create interesting jewelry with a natural look.

FACETED ROUNDS AND RONDELS

These shapes combine the versatility of round beads with the increased reflectivity created by faceting. Transparent gemstones are not the only ones that are faceted; opaque stones like black onyx and even, on occasion, the natural smooth round shapes of pearls can be faceted as well.

GEMSTONE BEAD SHAPES KEY

1. Onion-shaped briolettes (citrine)
2. Faceted discs (garnet)
3. Top-drilled marquise beads (peridot)
4. Faceted twisted box beads (labradorite)
5. Smooth round beads (golden rutilated quartz)
6. Flat faceted irregular beads (Sleeping Beauty Turquoise™)
7. Almond-shaped briolettes (rutilated quartz)
8. Faceted rondels (fire opal)
9. Faceted nuggets (Chinese turquoise)

CUTTING AND POLISHING

Pearls and a few gemstone crystals are attractive enough to be used in jewelry in their natural state, but the great majority of stones depend on the skills of cutters and polishers to make them into glittering gems. This process, which was traditionally and laboriously done by hand, is today accomplished with the assistance of partly automated or even fully automated machinery, but it still requires an expert understanding of the qualities of the gemstone. Gems can be destroyed or their looks cheapened by unskilled cutting, and decisions about how to achieve the greatest possible value from any piece of rough stone call for sophisticated judgment from cutters with many years of experience.

Many of the opaque and semitransparent stones are cut into rough shape and then turned on a lathe or in a ball mill to make them into round beads or domed cabochons. Then they are tumbled or polished so that their surface luster is revealed.

The true skill of cutting, however, is mainly practiced on the transparent stones that best display their optical qualities when they are faceted. Here, the gem maker must first decide which shapes to create on the basis of a balanced view of market demand and the most efficient way to use a particular piece of rough stone. Then he must determine the shape and number of facets that produce the most sparkle. Once he has arrived at a plan of action, each bead or stone must be cut individually. Despite the name "cutting," facets are actually created by wearing away the stone on a grinding wheel. With the exception of diamonds, which can only be ground by other diamonds, gems are faceted on a grinding wheel coated with carborundum, a synthetic form of the extremely hard gem moissanite. In the great gem cutting centers of India, some stones are still "hand-cut" using only traditional tools to help the eye guide the angles of the facets, but more and more gemstones are being "machine-cut" to achieve greater regularity and precision of both the facets and the overall size of the finished bead.

DROPS

Drop shapes are most often drilled sideways through the top or narrowest portion of the bead, but they can sometimes be found center-drilled where the hole traverses the entire length from top to bottom. The most common types of drops are teardrop or pear-shaped, almond, heart, onion, and marquise or double-ended. The last three shapes are flattened, presenting their widest aspect in two dimensions rather than three, and making the most economical use of the gem. Drops are as frequently faceted as rounds and in this more glittering state are often referred to as "briolettes." Another similar faceted shape is the "marquise," a type of drop pointed at both ends.

SPECIAL CUTS

The possibilities of faceting and shaping gemstones are still being explored and every year sees a creative new cut enter the marketplace. Some of these join the classic designs, whereas others enjoy a brief popularity in the ever-changing world of fashion.

CHIPS

Like sausages, chips are created from the leftovers after the main cuts have been removed. Cutting shapes from rough stone often involves wastage that, once sorted for size, tumble-polished, and drilled, is strung onto temporary strands and sold. And, like sausages, gemstone chips come in many different guises—some can be used for cheap and cheerful recipes, whereas others are sophisticated and serious elements of fine design.

VALUE

The value of gemstones is determined by several factors, primarily their popularity, rarity, and quality. With the exception of diamonds, which are subject to the controlling corporate influence of the De Beers group, prices are set by market demand. Because the market is so international, however, it is sometimes difficult to understand the causes of that demand; regional preferences play an important role in determining price, and gems tend to flow to the countries that value them most. A prime example of this is jade, which is fervently desired in China, but only modestly appreciated in the West. Few North Americans or Europeans can understand the fine gradations in quality or are willing to match the thousands of dollars that the Chinese are ready to spend on the best pieces. The sheer popularity of the stone among Chinese women pushes the prices of the best jade ever higher, while the women of the West, not so appreciative of the subtleties of this modest and discreet gem, are generally content to acquire the lesser qualities or give it a pass completely.

But popularity alone does not give value to gems—they must also be relatively rare, adding the problem of supply to the price equation. The variation in supply is enormous: some gems, such as Paraiba tourmaline, are found in the tiniest quantities in one or two places on earth, whereas others, to use the example of hematite (a form of iron oxide), are as common as rust. The consequence is that a single piece of the Paraiba tourmaline can cost as much as a house, whereas a nice strand of the hematite will set you back the price of a sandwich.

The most complex factor of value in gemstones, however, is quality. Even a relatively cheap type of gemstone can cost much more than an expensive one if its quality is superior. Because their livelihood depends on good judgment, dealers in gemstones have created sophisticated methods of measuring quality, methods that are often confusing and unhelpful to the layman who simply wants to purchase something that looks good. In my book *Simply Gemstones*, I describe some of the ways professionals look at gemstone beads to determine their quality and value, as well as a simple method anyone can use to quickly gain some insight into the important relationship of quality to price.

THE PRODUCTION OF GEMSTONES

Gemstones are mined on every continent except Antarctica, but some areas of the world are particularly rich in these resources. Brazil, Burma, India, Afghanistan, Russia, Sri Lanka, eastern and southern Africa, and North America all have large-scale production of rough gemstones. In the case of diamonds, vast corporate investments have created huge open pit mines hundreds of feet deep, fringed by industrial complexes that sift through millions of tons of rock. But most other gems are mined more modestly, often by hand, in makeshift pits or shafts. Some, such as the opal mines of Australia are the territory of rugged individual treasure seekers, others are the enterprise of modern mining companies, and still others remain the traditional livelihood of remote communities. However the raw stone is wrenched from the ground, few gems are processed in the place they are mined. The rough gemstone is loaded into containers or barrels and shipped to the cutters and polishers of Europe and Asia. In recent years the former has been eclipsed by the latter, and even diamonds, once faceted in the workshops of Amsterdam and Antwerp, are now mostly cut in India. Traditional centers of gem cutting, such as Jaipur and Bangkok, still have thriving industries, but China, the leader in pearl production, has become the main producer of smooth round stones and is rapidly increasing its production of faceted stones. This vast international network of miners, cutters, and dealers offers today's jewelry designer an immense choice of gemstones in myriad shapes and sizes at many levels of quality and price.

GEMSTONE NAMES

Creating a list of gemstones is often a confusing business as many of them are known by two or more names. Compounding the difficulty is the fact that many seemingly unique gems are simply different aspects of one material.

1

2

3

4

5

6

7

8

9

10

11

12

13

14

For example, sapphires and rubies are both a gemstone called "corundum," a crystalline form of aluminum oxide. The only difference between them is that rubies are red corundum, whereas sapphires can be of many other colors. Jade, thought to be just one type of gemstone for thousands of years, was shown in the nineteenth century to be two separate minerals, jadeite and nephrite. Members of the garnet group don't even share the same chemical composition, although they all adhere to the same cubic crystalline structure and have similar hardness. Onyx, agate, and chalcedony are all quartz, as are the stones that are actually called quartz. Even the agreed names for stones have variations in spelling—some refer to one familiar form of garnet as "almandine," others say "almandite."

And added to all the variations of scientific and traditional names are the myriad titles bestowed on stones by sellers trying to make them sound more attractive. Thus, serpentine is commonly called "new jade" or "soo chow jade"; metallic pyrite, diminished by its nickname of "fool's gold," is often called "marcasite" even though that is the name of a completely different mineral; "Umba" sapphire really is a type of sapphire discovered in Africa's Umba River valley; "tundra" sapphire is neither found in the tundra, nor is it sapphire, but a particular color mixture of several other types of gemstone; and "water sapphire" is just a more romantic name for indicolite, a blue tourmaline. Even correct names can confuse. Peruvian opal is, indeed, a "hydrous silica gel" like its more precious cousin, but it has no play-of-color and no fire—in fact, it doesn't look the slightest bit like anyone's idea of opal. Then there are the blatantly false names, meant to confuse. Bohemian ruby for garnet, smoky topaz for smoky quartz, cherry quartz for glass, African emerald for green fluorite. It is enough to make one wish for some single authority to impose order. But sometimes the trade name is simply much better than the mineral name; we can all be thankful that someone had the bright idea of giving oligoclase feldspar the name *sunstone*, which delightfully describes its appearance. In the end, the market somehow arrives at the goal of assigning attractive names to beautiful gemstones, occasionally sidestepping a little confusion and deception along the way.

GEMSTONE BEAD SHAPES KEY
Opposite Page
 1. Slice pendant (Chinese turquoise)
 2. Faceted box (Swiss blue topaz)
 3. Briolette (rose quartz)
 4. Laser cut drop (garnet)
 5. Laser cut flat drop (London blue topaz)
 6. Large disc pendant (banded agate)
 7. Carved leaf (serpentine)
 8. Faceted chiclet (amethyst)
 9. Cabochon set in silver pendant (aquamarine)
10. Faceted almond (labradorite)
11. Carved fish (carnelian)
12. Large faceted pendant (blue goldstone)
13. Carved flattened barrel (amethyst)
14. Center-drilled flat-bottomed drop (lemon citrine)

There are several hundred gemstones, many of which, due to their fragility or extreme rareness, are only of interest to collectors. The following chart describes most of the gemstones that are used in jewelry and are currently available in the marketplace as beads or pendants.

GEMSTONE	HARDNESS	COLOR(S)	REMARKS
agate	7	banded—many colors	commonly dyed
almandine (garnet)	7	red with a violet tinge	sometimes with a slight metallic luster
amazonite	6	blue-green	silky luster
amber	2	yellow-brown	resinous luster; often imitated by natural and synthetic resins
amethyst	7	purple	also heat-treated to create green amethyst
ammonite	4	brown with iridescence	the fossilized shells of extinct sea creatures
andalusite	7	brown-red, yellow-green	changes color in different light
apatite	5	green, blue, yellow	
aquamarine	8	blue, blue-green	heat-treated to achieve the best colors
aventurine	7	green to gold-brown	can be confused with "goldstone," a glass simulant
black onyx	7	black	a black type of chalcedony
bloodstone	7	dark green with red spots	
carnelian	7	orange, red-brown	vitreous to waxy luster; mostly dyed and/or heat-treated
chalcedony	7	blue, gray, white	other colors created through dyeing
charoite	5	violet with white veins	
chrysocolla	2	mottled green-blue and brown	vitreous to greasy luster
chrysoprase	7	apple green	vitreous to waxy luster
citrine	7	yellow, yellow-gold	most citrine is heat-treated amethyst
coral	3	red, black, white, and dyed colors	vitreous to dull luster; some varieties raise environmental concerns
cubic zirconia	8	many colors	a synthetic sometimes used to imitate diamond; very dense and heavy
diamond	10	colorless, black, brown, yellow, green	adamantine luster and brilliant fire
diopside	5	green	can be confused with emerald
druse	7	clear and other colors	crystalline interior of a hollow agate
emerald	8	green	usually oiled to improve surface; often clouded with inclusions
fire agate	7	orange-white with iridescence	
fluorite	4	mostly purple, but many other colors, often banded	
garnet	7	red	
grossular (garnet)	7	green	
hematite	6	gray-black	metallic luster; almost all hematite is reconstituted
hessonite (garnet)	7	syrupy brown	vitreous to resinous luster
howlite	3	white with black veins	porous and easily dyed; used to imitate turquoise
hypersthene	5	dark green	
indicolite	7	deep blue	a type of blue tourmaline
iolite	7	blue	
jade (jadeite & nephrite)	7	green, white, lilac	greasy to pearly luster; imitated by serpentine
jasper	7	many colors, striped, spotted or patterned	
jet	2	black	waxy luster; a form of coal
kunzite	7	lilac	

Note: Hardness indicates the approximate position on the Mohs scale of hardness. Stones with a higher hardness number scratch any of the ones below them in the scale. Glass has a hardness of 5 and any stones below that are considered to be "soft"; those of 8 or greater are very hard stones.

GEMSTONE	HARDNESS	COLOR(S)	REMARKS
kyanite	4 & 6	blue with streaks	vitreous to pearly luster
labradorite	6	gray-black with iridescence	best has a strong blue-green schiller
lapis lazuli	5	blue with brassy specks	vitreous to greasy luster; best is from Afghanistan; Chilean lapis is often dyed; the stone is imitated by sodalite and even glass
larimar (pectolite)	5	blue with white veins	best quality has more blue, less white
malachite	4	banded dark and light green	vitreous to silky
moonstone	6	white with blue or white opalescence	sometimes imitated by glass
morganite	7	pink	also called pink beryl or aquamarine
obsidian	5	black	a naturally occurring volcanic form of glass
opal (common)	6	blue, pink	same stone as opal, but without the play-of-color
opal (precious)	6	white or black with iridescence	vulnerable to drying and cracking
pearl	3	white, cream, golden, black and others	almost all are cultured; many are bleached or dyed
peridot	6	green	vitreous to greasy luster
prehnite	6	yellow-green	
pyrite	6	bronze-gold	metallic luster; called marcasite when set in silver
pyrope (garnet)	7	deep red	
rhodochrosite	4	pink with white veins	vitreous to pearly luster
rhodonite	6	pink with black veins	
rock crystal	7	clear	often sold in natural crystal shapes
rose quartz	7	cloudy pink	often dyed to improve the color
ruby	9	red	often dyed to improve the color
ruby zoisite	6	green with red inclusions	
rutilated quartz	7	clear with gold, black or red inclusions	the hairlike rutile is an opaque gemstone
sapphire	9	many colors except red	heat treatment produces a variety of colors
serpentine	5	green	vitreous to greasy luster; many trade names implying it is jade, which it is not
smoky quartz	7	brown-gray	
sodalite	5	blue with white veins	vitreous to greasy luster
spessartine (garnet)	7	orange-red	
spinel	8	black, red, blue	red spinel is sometimes sold as ruby
sugilite	6	violet	
sunstone	6	red-brown	
tanzanite	6	blue with purple and violet overtones	blue form of zoisite
tiger's-eye	7	brown-gold with chatoyancy	red tiger's-eye is dyed
topaz	8	yellow-brown, pink, blue, green	most pink and blue topaz has been heat-treated
tourmaline	7	many colors	
tsavorite	7	green	transparent form of green grossular garnet
turquoise	5	blue, green	waxy to dull luster; sometimes impregnated with resin (stabilized), sometimes oiled, sometimes reconstituted; imitated by dyed howlite; good synthetics are available; the stone is often faked
vesuvianite (idocrase)	6	green-brown	greasy luster
zircon	7	colorless, blue, yellow, red, brown, green	vitreous to adamantine luster

CARING FOR GEMSTONES

For all their hardness and solidity, gemstones can be vulnerable to the stresses of daily life and need to be properly protected. All gems can break and all, except diamonds, can be scratched. Sometimes the dulling of a stone's surface can be caused by nothing more than the insidious nature of seemingly innocent influences. Although we think of dust as a soft and gentle substance, much of it is composed of tiny quartz particles that have a hardness of 7 on the Mohs scale (Hardness, page 211) and will scratch any softer stone. All gemstone jewelry should be kept in a protective bag, whether it is of soft cloth or simple plastic. Do not throw your gems into a heap in your jewelry box, for one will almost surely scratch another. Rather than trying to remember which gemstones break easily, it is better to realize that they all break and to keep them away from work or sports activities that might cause them harm.

The rays of the sun can cause the colors of some stones, like old soldiers, to simply fade away. While it is easy to understand that enhanced stones are sometimes subject to color deterioration, it is not commonly understood that many natural gemstones are also susceptible. Yet stones like amethyst, chalcedony, coral, and kunzite can all fade in simple daylight. So, unless they are diamonds, don't wear gems during a lengthy sunbathing session and, if you live in a hot, sunny climate, any stones vulnerable to color change should be saved for indoor or evening wear.

Even water can be a threat. Opaque, noncrystalline stones are porous and will happily suck up water and any nasty chemicals dissolved in it. Don't jump in the hot tub or shower with your jewelry on. Don't do the dishes wearing a gemstone bracelet. Don't go swimming in your pearls—they come from the sea, and their little calcium carbonate hearts would love to dissolve back into the ocean. But, while gemstones are better kept out of water, many of them depend on the stuff and suffer if they dry out, so keep your jewelry in a place that has at least a little humidity—it won't hurt any of them and will soothe those like opals and pearls that fear drying out.

Some gems are easily damaged by acids, cosmetics, hair sprays, and so on, so it is safest, for all gemstone jewelry, to use the old adage for pearls, "Put them on last and take them off first." This way they are less likely to receive a gratuitous shower of hair spray or perfume.

CLEANING GEMSTONES

If you use the guidelines above for wearing and storing your gemstones, they should remain in their pristine state for a very long time. Unfortunately the same cannot be said for the silver and low-karat gold that might accompany them. Tarnish needs to be removed, and gemstones can make that a difficult task. A few gems, such as rubies, sapphires, and diamonds, can stand being plunged into liquid silver and gold cleaners, but the great majority cannot. So, do not even think about it! (If your rubies contain any color-enhancing dye, you will certainly find out about it when they are bathed in chemicals, and you will wish you had not.) Ultrasonic cleaners might allow the very hardest gems to survive, but you are taking a chance putting anything less than diamonds, sapphires, and rubies into them—so don't.

A better method for cleaning is to treat the precious metals and the gemstones separately. Use a silver or gold cleaning cloth to remove tarnish from the metallic elements, then clean the gemstones with a very soft toothbrush dipped in a weak solution of water and very mild soap. Pat them dry with an absorbent towel. Think of the metallic bits as teenagers who can only benefit from a good scrubbing and the gemstones as babies whose tender skin demands the gentlest of care.

SOME STONES THAT REQUIRE EXTRA SPECIAL CARE

Opals: Soft and containing significant amounts of water, opals are among the most delicate of gemstones. Great care should be taken to avoid an environment where they will dry out, for they will crack and lose their beauty. Opals are notorious for falling out of their settings, breaking, and losing their color; storing in moist absorbent cotton is often advised.

Turquoise: The natural color of the stone can be changed by heat, strong light, and cosmetics and detergents. Turquoise is both porous and water-containing, so it can absorb damaging liquids, and drying out can cause cracking. The stone is relatively soft and easily scratched.

Amber and jet: Since it is a fossilized tree resin, amber is extremely soft and can be scratched by a fingernail. It is sensitive to heat and can be burned, like incense, by the flame of a simple match. Acids, alcohol, and many other chemicals can cause damage. Jet is similar to amber in vulnerability.

Coral and pearls: These are both soft and vulnerable to scratching. Composed of calcium carbonate, they will dissolve in acids. Store them carefully and keep them away from chemicals and polluted air.

Lapis lazuli: This stone is sensitive to chemicals, hot water, acid, and alkali. Keep it away when performing household chores.

Chrysacolla, rhodochrosite, malachite, and howlite: Are all soft and easily scratched.

Tourmaline: Has the strange quality of attracting dust and dirt when it is rubbed or heated. Keep it in a protective pouch and wipe it clean more frequently than other gems.

RESOURCES

If you are interested in learning more about the story of these fascinating metals, the following websites contain general information and links:

The Silver Institute   www.silverinstitue.org
World Gold Council   www.gold.org

The following websites are well worth visiting if only to see their beautiful examples of the finest pearls and faux pearls:

www.paspaleypearls.com (for South Sea pearls)
www.mikimoto.com (for Akoya pearls)
www.perlesdetahiti.net (for Tahitian black pearls)
www.americanpearlcompany.com (for American freshwater peals)
www.create-your-style.com (for faux pearls)

For information about Swarovski Crystal products:
www.create-your-style.com

There are many wonderful glass bead artists who have their works exhibited online with details about where to find them:
Alena and Alex Chladkova, www.aleale.cz
Leah Fairbanks, www.leahfairbanks.com
Kate Fowle Meleney, www.katefowle.com
Kristen Frantzen Orr, www.kristenfrantzenorr.com
Susan Knopp, www.susanknoppenamels.com
Kevin O'Grady, www.kevinogrady.com
Nancy Pilgrim, www.nancypilgrim.com
Cynthia Liebler Saari, www.clsaari.com

Many of the materials for these designs, as well as the locations of Beadworks stores, can be found online at www.beadworks.com.

There are several Internet directories of bead stores, including www.guidetobeadwork.com. The website www.mapmuse.com quickly finds a bead store location near you if you go to "crafts" and then to "beading shops."

A number of publications serve the bead customer and have large resource listings:

Bead & Button Magazine: www.beadandbutton.com

Beadwork Magazine: www.interweave.com/bead/beadwork_magazine

Bead Style: www.beadstylemag.com

For information or further education about gemstones, the following sites might be of interest:

The Gemological Institute of America: www.gia.edu

The Gemmological Association of Great Britain: www.gem-a.info

The Gemmological Association of Australia: www.gem.org.au

The Smithsonian, National Gem and Mineral Collection: www.mineralsciences.si.edu/collections.htm

American Gem Trade Association: www.agta.org

Due to the rapid growth of bead stores in the past twenty years, there is now a wide selection of places to buy beads, findings, and threading materials. In North America alone, there are more than a thousand bead stores, as well as dozens of Internet retailers. Although shopping online can be quick and convenient, nothing beats the experience of being in a well-stocked bead store. There you are able to feel the texture of the beads and arrange them side by side to see if the combinations please you. If you cannot find exactly the bead you are looking for, don't be afraid of making suitable substitutions for materials in the designs. By adding some of your own creative judgment, you end up with a piece of jewelry that is uniquely yours.

ABOUT THE AUTHOR

Nancy Alden is a jewelry designer and cofounder of the Beadworks Group, one of the world's largest retailers of beads. As Beadworks' principal buyer and designer, she has traveled the world in search of the most beautiful components for jewelry design. She is as at home with gemstone merchants in Jaipur, silver makers in Bali, and glass artists in Bohemia as she is with pearl producers in China. Her knowledge of beads and findings is unrivaled, spanning all categories of material and all stages of production, from the creation of a single bead to its final role in a finished piece of jewelry.

Starting as a silver and goldsmith, Nancy turned to designing with beads because of the vastly greater possibilities for creative expression. Having seen the world of jewelry design open for herself, she then went on to introduce other people to the creative pleasures and the economies of making their own jewelry. By creating Beadworks classes and sharing her skills with other instructors, she has generated a network of teachers who have added to the ever-growing number of women and men able to design and create jewelry. When she is not in search of new beads, Nancy divides her time between her home in Connecticut and her studio retreats in Europe and the Grenadines.

ABOUT BEADWORKS

In 1978, a small store in London began selling a very ancient product in a very novel way. Although beads are among the very earliest of traded articles, the concept of offering a large, sophisticated, and open display to the general public was new. The shop never advertised—indeed, it didn't even have a name for many years—but the demand for its products was immediate and overwhelming. Simply by word of mouth, the original store became world famous. With American jewelry designer Nancy Alden, the concept expanded to North America, where it has grown to half a dozen stores and a mail-order business. Beadworks has inspired people from around the world to open their own bead stores, enabling hundreds of thousands of people to make their own jewelry. You can visit Beadworks online at www.beadworks.com.

INDEX

SIMPLY STUNNING JEWELRY